RULED BY THE SPIRIT

BASILEA SCHLINK

Translated by

John and Mary Foote

and

Michael Harper

LAKELAND
MARSHALL, MORGAN & SCOTT
116 BAKER STREET
LONDON W1M2BB

First British Edition 1970
Reprinted 1971
Reprinted 1972
Reprinted 1975

ISBN 0 551 00207 7

Printed in Great Britain by
Cox & Wyman Ltd, London, Reading and Fakenham

579011R51

Contents

1 *The Wind of the Spirit*

Astonishing news has reached us recently from Indonesia.[1] Powerful spiritual currents are flowing in unprecedented ways through this "kingdom of the thousand islands". Revival broke out during the autumn of 1965 on a whole string of islands and thousands of Indonesians have come to a living faith in Jesus. A church newsletter reported that forty thousand heathen, and as many nominal Christians, have been won for Jesus. On the island of Timor there are scarcely any heathen left. In the principal town the prisons are almost empty. In the Amfoang district, once known as a bastion of the devil, where for fifty years Church and government have fought a futile battle against drunkenness, black magic, sorcery and idolatry, nearly ten thousand people have abandoned their occult practices.

Eye-witnesses have explained this remarkable transformation as the collapse of the devil's strongholds through the mighty power of the Holy Spirit. God's Spirit began to work in individuals. A peasant woman who had been back-sliding returned to Jesus in deep repentance as a result of a vision. Following this spiritual experience she felt a burning sense of commission to deliver others from the powers of darkness. This simple woman

7

brought one of the first Gospel teams into existence. A young Christian, afflicted for a time with blindness and lameness through compromise with secret occult practices, experienced the withdrawal of God's chastening hand when he confessed them. He felt he had to witness to the congregation about this experience of the holiness of God. God's Spirit used this witness to produce a deep awareness of sin which caused many more to repent.

This breathing of the Holy Spirit caused many relentlessly to attack sin. It also created new boldness in witness and sacrificial love. Soon seventy-two Gospel teams linked up right across the country. In less than two years they had grown to one hundred and fifty teams, almost a thousand people in action for Jesus. Many are simple rice-growing farmers; some are illiterate. They include women too. Their sacrificial love and the authority with which they proclaim the Gospel are given to them by the Holy Spirit, who confirms their action with signs following.

In particular the Lord has endowed a number of groups with the ministry of healing. Thousands of sick people have been made well. One such group, known as the "fire team", was given such power by the Holy Spirit that God revealed Himself through their simple testimony as "consuming fire", and as a result those who would not give up their evil ways experienced terrible suffering. Wrestling for the souls of men is always the driving force of these Gospel teams. The Holy Spirit's power kindles their sacrificial love, so that they have no peace until the lost are delivered from sin. Today it is again the Spirit's power that lifts people from the abyss, changes their lives and gives them new strength. The power which changes people and enables them to serve others through prayer and sacrificial love is always that of the Holy Spirit.

There was once a nation which fell away from God; it became greedy and worshipped the golden calf. Aaron, God's choice for High Priest, let himself be ruled by the will of the people and be carried away by the crowd. They indulged in sinful practices without restraint, and so God's sentence was passed, for "sin is a reproach to any people" (Prov. 14:34). Judgment follows upon sin which cries out to heaven.

When the dance around the golden calf provoked the sentence of destruction upon the nation, it was stayed by the sacrificial love of an intercessor, who was fully empowered by the Holy Spirit. He was able to move the heart of God so that He again withdrew His arm stretched out in judgment. The nation was chastened but not destroyed. Moses was the name of this priestly intercessor. He was the deliverer of his people; through his intercession the severe threats of judgment were once more withdrawn and mercy was shown to the people.

We live in a similar situation today. Once more people dance around the golden calf. It is a time of apostasy. God is declared to be dead and people revel in sin. Even voices from the Christian world encourage sin by watering down God's commandments. The spread of lawlessness is indeed the characteristic of our age (Matt. 24:12). The open and hitherto unprecedented glorification of sin has resulted in an alarming increase in crime, especially in sexual offences. Among young people it has resulted in the formation of gangs and groups of criminals, and in the increasing loss of self-control. Not only our nation, but every nation is today threatened with judgment. We face the greatest destruction the earth has seen since the flood—a judgment of fire (2 Pet. 3:10).

The great stockpiles of nuclear weapons are constantly increasing. The existing stock far exceeds the quantity needed to obliterate human life on the earth. Now, sooner than Western military experts had expected, China has produced and exploded hydrogen bombs. Behind all this is the sinister power of hatred—waiting to break out in war. China has said that the loss of a few hundred million lives would not matter, as their own country is, in any case, over-populated. The smouldering ashes of war and the constantly recurring crises in world politics bring near the time when the world will go up in flames. This likelihood has been clearly demonstrated by the recent developments of war in the Middle East.

This threat of nuclear war cannot, as many think, be averted by political action. Behind it stands God's very real threat of judgment upon a world of apostasy and sin. What can delay such destruction, so that many may still be saved? Only men like Moses can command such a situation— men who hate sin, regarding it as an insult to God—as something horrible and ugly, mean and frightful, bringing ruin and destruction. Moses could not watch his people being ruined and destroyed by sin. In raging fury he took merciless action against this sin in the power of the Spirit. On the day of God's judgment, three thousand were killed in the Israelite camp. At the same time

Moses stands before God with the one heartfelt desire, implanted by the Holy Spirit, to save and save again. It is the fiery Spirit of love which enables him to love his people, who only a few weeks earlier wanted to stone him to death. He loves them so much that he offers himself to God and asks Him to blot the name of Moses out of the book of life if only the people might be saved.

In the New Testament we see the apostle Paul, similarly filled with the Holy Spirit and full of zeal and burning love for the souls of men. Paul is ready to have his name crossed out of the book of life in order that some of his nation might be saved (Rom. 9:3). But in the New Testament, unlike the Old, it is not only a few outstanding personalities who are singled out to receive the sacrificial love of the Holy Spirit. Since Jesus has come and ascended to heaven, all believers are called to serve in the Church and to be used for the salvation of the world. The Holy Spirit has been promised to all (Acts 2:39). The accounts in Acts show how the whole Church was equipped with the power and authority of the Holy Spirit. Thus, mighty acts were performed among the believers—miracles and signs in the power of the Holy Spirit. By these acts the Church of God was built up and men were saved from the powers of darkness.

This truth is still valid today. The Holy Spirit is ready to work effectively throughout the Church. How does this relate to our world situation, which is so much more serious than that of New Testament times? Is the Church of Christ, empowered by the Holy Spirit, really moving God through prayer in a spirit of compassion as she hears the death-cry of the world? Is she filled with

11

the Holy Spirit, who gives authority to men, in order to halt, at least here and there, the power of the devil? Where are those people, like Moses and Paul, who are prepared to offer themselves as a sacrifice, because their whole being is on fire with love, so that at least a few may be saved? Where are those whose hearts resound with the one word: "save"? In these last days our world is waiting for them, for they alone have the power to prevent its destruction.

But for the most part we are like those who are asleep: "there were very many bones in the valley and behold they were very dry . . . our bones are dried up, and our hope is lost; we are clear cut off" (Ezek. 37:2,11). As in those days, there is only one who can help us. God's Spirit must come down upon us and blow through us. "I will cause breath to enter you, and you shall live" (Ezek. 37:5). When we claim this promise and begin to beg and pray, then we shall experience the life-giving action of the Holy Spirit.

Our world has never been in such great danger as it is today. This is why we must strive for the outpouring of the Spirit. To a great extent spiritual life is stunted, because people are satisfied with having a relationship with Jesus, or at the most with Jesus and the Father. The power of the Holy Spirit is not being taken seriously enough. Our personal relationship with Him is rudimentary. The spiritual life of both the individual and the Church suffers. If we do not ask for the Holy Spirit and call upon Him for His gifts, we shall be missing something crucial, for He will be unable to give all that the Scriptures tell us He has in store for us. Thus Johann Christoph Blumhardt, moved by the misery of those who sought his spiritual advice, cried out: "let us pray and hope for a new outpouring of the Holy Spirit. It must come, if the level of our Christian living is to change. We cannot go on in this miserable way. Those first gifts and powers are meant to return, and I believe that our dear Lord is only waiting for us to pray for them".[2]

So it is our task to pray for the Holy Spirit in our times, which bear the signs of the last days. These signs include — increasing lawlessness (Matt. 24:12), the threat of nuclear war (with the possibility of the fulfilment of all the visions of Revelation) and the preaching of the Gospel throughout the world (Matt. 24:14).

In this world situation of the last days the Church should be experiencing a much greater fulness of the powers and gifts of the Holy Spirit. She must be equipped to fight against the satanic powers and the Antichrist himself. This is why a special outpouring of the Holy Spirit is promised for the last days. "And in the last days it shall come to pass that I will pour out my Spirit upon all flesh . . ." (Joel 2:28ff, Acts 2:17). This promise was wonderfully fulfilled at Pentecost, but will have its final fulfilment in this age.

Without being specially equipped by the Holy Spirit, it would be presumptuous to believe ourselves capable of opposing the mighty satanic forces and powers of deception in the last days. If the disciples had thought that they had all they needed in Jesus Christ and had not waited for the Holy Spirit to equip them, they would not have been able to stand victoriously in a world which relentlessly opposed and persecuted them. The mighty deeds of God, which we read about in the New Testament, would not have happened. The disciples would never have gone as witnesses to Jesus "to the ends of the earth". So too we need the Holy Spirit if we are to resist Satan, hold our ground against every kind of persecution and pressure, and enable others to hear the good news of salvation. Only with the help of the Holy Spirit will we be able to serve "in demonstration of the Spirit and power" (1 Cor. 2:4).

2 *The Promised One has Come*

Jesus left behind grief-stricken disciples fearful of not being able to stand against the threats of their persecutors. Yet He says to them: "It is to your advantage that I go away" (John 16:7). How could it be advantageous to the disciples for Jesus to leave them? He meant everything to them and they were utterly dependent on Him. Could there be any greater loss than the loss of Jesus for those to whom He meant everything? And yet Jesus says: it is good for you that I leave you! It is good for you to suffer this loss! And then He goes on to explain to them why it is to their advantage. He tells them that something great will take place when He has gone away, and He says that emphatically—He says: "I tell you the truth."

Now, when He who is the second Person of the Trinity leaves this world, the third Person of the Godhead, the Holy Spirit, will come to His people to dwell in them. So Jesus says to them, "I will send you another Comforter" (John 14:16). In His place another, even the Holy Spirit, will now comfort them. The greek word for Comforter is *parakletos*. This word is made up of the word "para", which means "side by side", and "kletos", which means "one who is called". Thus the whole word means: "One who is called to stand alongside

15

another"—to be beside another person and to help him in every need.

Until then the disciples had been able to turn to Jesus at any time with their problems; but now they are to turn to the Holy Spirit for help and counsel. However, they were not to be separated from Jesus Christ, because He is ever present through the Holy Spirit—the Holy Trinity is indivisibly whole. The Holy Spirit is at one and the same time the Spirit of God as well as God's means of making His presence known and glorifying Himself in the world. He is also the Spirit of Jesus Christ and the means whereby the ascended Lord extends His kingdom in this age and awakens belief in Himself. By leading us to believe in Jesus, the Holy Spirit makes us children of God and leads us to pray "Abba, Father!" (Rom. 8:14-15).

But while Father, Son and Spirit are a unity, in which the Holy Spirit is both the bond of love and the power which goes forth from the Father and the Son, the scriptures and creeds of the Church witness to the fact that the Holy Spirit is a Person in company with the Father and the Son. This is particularly clear in those passages in the New Testament which speak of the relationship of the believer to the Holy Spirit. For example, we are told that the Holy Spirit exhorts us. Just as the Father calls us, demanding our obedience, and the Lord Jesus does the same in calling us to follow Him, so the Holy Spirit also calls us and exhorts us to follow His leadings. It is He who teaches and reminds the disciples (John 14:26). He leads them into perfect truth (John 16:8). It is He who convicts their hearts and consciences of sin (John 16:8) It is He who gives Christians the

16

ability to witness for Jesus (John 15:26, 27). It is He who calls us to service (Acts 13:2), and He it is who sends us out (Acts 8:29; 13:4). He checks us and does not allow those whom He sends to do anything contrary to God's plan (Acts 16:6,7). Just as the Father and the Son lead us, so also does the Holy Spirit guide us. It is our privilege to be led by Him and we should let Him guide us. (Gal. 5:18; Heb. 10:29).

The Holy Spirit then is the Third Person of the Trinity, full of majesty and glory, holiness and power, and ready to take possession of people and use them as His instruments. He is not an "atmosphere" which is at our disposal, even though He is both a gift from God and power from on high. The Spirit is a gift which a man may receive; but it is the Spirit who is Lord of that man. God keeps command of the Spirit, His Gift. "The wind blows where it wills . . ." (John 3:8). The almighty and divine will and the declaration of it belong particularly to the third Person of the Trinity, the Holy Spirit, as we find in 1 Cor. 12:11: "And these are inspired by one and the same Spirit, who apportions to each one individually as He wills".

Because of all this, the Holy Spirit is to be worshipped, as we say in the Nicene Creed, as the "Lord and giver of life, who proceedeth from the Father and the Son, who with the Father and the Son together is worshipped and glorified, who spake by the prophets"

It is, then, the Holy Spirit who leads us, calls us, comforts us, equips us and gives us strength. Words are not adequate to express our praise and thanks. He manifests our Lord Jesus clearly to us, reminds

17

us of Him, warns us, restrains us when we want to take the wrong path, comforts us, loves us and accomplishes great actions through us. He should be thanked and worshipped every day as He leads us in His restoring love, and strengthens us for prayer, supplication, faith and service.

Jesus' love and concern are overwhelming, for He did not leave His followers to be orphans when he departed from this earth but sent the Holy Spirit to them. The Holy Spirit is able to help us just as lovingly and powerfully today as then. He is always with us, because He lives in our hearts. Furthermore, He joins us together in the "fellowship of the Holy Spirit" (2 Cor. 13:14). What a guest we have in the Holy Spirit! What an important and divine person! The old Whitsun hymns speak of Him as the One with wonderful names. He is the Spirit of widsom, of counsel and of understanding (Isa.11:2). He is the Spirit of truth (John 14:17). He comes as the Spirit of comfort (John 14:26); and He is the Spirit of life (Rom. 8:2). He is the Spirit of holiness (Psa.51:11:13); He is the Spirit of faith (2 Cor. 4:13). He is the Spirit of power (2 Tim. 1:7). He is the Spirit of grace (Heb. 10:29), opening for us the treasure-house of God's love. He, like the Father and the Son, is full of glory—the Spirit of glory (1 Pet. 4:14). He is the Spirit of revelation (Eph. 1:17) and the Spirit of love (2 Tim. 1:7).

The Holy Spirit comes to us as helper and guide, to bring forth the fruit of the Spirit and to bestow upon us the gifts that we need. Everyone who receives this Spirit is to be counted amongst the blessed. Even an earthly guest, a human being, can transform a whole house by the influence of his love and joy when he helps and advises us in our need. But such transformations are even more effective when the most important visitor, the Holy Spirit, comes to us as the Spirit of joy, love, counsel, comfort, mercy and life. (The effect of His visit can be gauged by what we are told about the disciples when they received Him.)

How important it is to know about His work within the Trinity! To some extent the triune God revealed Himself in this manner in the Old Testament. For we are told that Abraham saw the day of Christ (John 8:56). We are also told that the Psalms and prophets spoke of Him (Luke 24:44; Psa.22;Is.53). But not until the fullness of time was come, did Jesus really come to His people on earth. So it is with the Holy Spirit. God's Spirit was at work in the Old Testament, for in the building of the tabernacle the craftsmen were "filled with the Spirit of God" (Exod.31:3;35:31). Of the seventy elders at Sinai we are told that the Spirit of God rested on them and they prophesied (Num. 11:25). The Spirit of the Lord came upon David at his anointing (1 Sam. 16:13), and the prophets experienced this too—for instance, Ezekiel says: "the Spirit of the Lord fell upon me" (Ezek. 11:5). The Spirit of God was also at work in the time of Jesus. Simeon came to the Temple at the bidding of the Holy Spirit (Luke 2:27). The Holy Spirit came upon Jesus Himself (Luke 3:22). Jesus drove the devil away by the power of the Spirit (Matt.12:28). But it was not until Jesus had gone away that the full dispensation of the Holy Spirit began in the New Testament Church. It was then that He was given with the plentitude of His

19

gifts.

Jesus tells us that the period of time between His ascension and return is particularly the age of the Holy Spirit so far as the Christian Church is concerned, and we are in that age now. Jesus has entrusted the Holy Spirit with His Church for this period. It is crucial for the Church to grasp this fact and receive the Holy Spirit if it is to live the Spirit-filled life in the service of God. It is impossible for the Church of Christ to say "I have Jesus and that is enough for me". We must bear in mind that we can only have Jesus if we are open to the work of the Holy Spirit. For the ascended Lord has expressly bequeathed His Church to the Holy Spirit. The accounts of the Acts of the Apostles confirm that this is true. The mighty missionary expansion, the signs and miracles performed by the apostles and others, and everything that happened amongst the mass of believers, are all acts of the Holy Spirit. Through His influence a Church developed which was endowed with the gifts of the Spirit, and which manifested them in a vigorous congregational life.

3 *These Men are Turning the World Upside Down*

We read in the Acts of the Apostles a clear, impressive description of how the disciples of Jesus received the Holy Spirit. On the day of Pentecost they were all gathered together with one accord, awaiting the Holy Spirit. He came like the rush of a mighty wind and they were filled with Him and endowed with His gifts. It was as if a great flame had enveloped them and set them on fire. They became living torches. It is almost incomprehensible that the Holy Spirit could so suddenly transform them into men of authority. In the power of the Spirit words poured from their mouths. They had become witnesses. Their words were full of wisdom. God's purposes for the future, revelations of His wisdom, and the plan of salvation were made known to them, and then revealed through them to the people.

In the witness of the disciples it is immediately clear that Father, Son and Holy Spirit are One. For when Jesus began His ministry the one message He preached throughout the land was: "Repent, for the kingdom of heaven is at hand!" And now we find the addresses of the Spirit-filled disciples have one and the same aim: "Repent!" This is true of the preaching of Peter, Stephen and Paul, even when the latter preached to pagans in Athens.

Those who have received the Holy Spirit preach the same gospel, which Jesus and His forerunner, John the Baptist, had already proclaimed—"repent, for the kingdom of heaven is at hand" (Matt. 3:2). John had been filled with the Holy Spirit in his mother's womb.

The disciples, through their encounter with the Holy Spirit, came to know Jesus, crucified because of their sin, in a completely new way. A radically new love for Him was kindled in them resulting in a fiery hatred of sin. Like Phinehas (Num.25), they were zealous that hidden sin might be brought to light, as in the case of Ananias and Sapphira. It is the task of the Holy Spirit to convict of sin (John 16:8). Working as the Spirit of light, He glorifies Jesus, for whenever sin is brought to light, His act of love which has redeemed us from all evil shines forth in splendour and radiance. Whenever the witnesses empowered by the Holy Spirit are at work testifying to Jesus they always proclaim the call to repentance and bring about change of heart.

Therefore, the apostles, who at Pentecost had received authority from the Holy Spirit and were themselves living in daily repentance, had to call sin mercilessly by its real name and openly condemn it. Peter said unequivocally to the people: "This Jesus you crucified and killed by the hands of lawless men" (Acts 2:23). And again: "Let the house of Israel, therefore, know assuredly that God has made Him both Lord and Christ, this Jesus whom you crucified" (Acts 2:36). In such words Peter is saying to his countrymen with unmistakable candour—you are guilty, all of you, even if you did not personally call out "crucify Him!" For you did nothing to prevent it, and you share in the guilt of the crucifixion of Jesus because you were too cowardly and indifferent.

The apostles even dared openly to accuse the Sanhedrin, so on fire were they against evil, even though the name of Jesus was very offensive to them: "Jesus of Nazareth whom *you* crucified . . ." they said (Acts 4:10). Stephen also was courageous enough to call sin uncompromisingly by its name, although for him it became a matter of life *and death*.

The first witnesses were able to do such things fearlessly, because the promised Holy Spirit had come to them. They learned to see sin clearly and to have a right attitude towards it. They made no excuses for it. They did not make the mistake of acting benevolently on the ground that the people had been unable to recognise Jesus' Messiahship because He had not taken a strong line of action, but rather had allowed Himself to be bound, condemned and crucified. Nor did they accept the argument that the people had to believe their spiritual leaders and obey them—even when the leaders had wrongly taught about Jesus of Nazareth and expected the people to join in their opposition of Him. There is not the slightest suggestion that the disciples accepted any diminishing of the people's responsibility or their guilt in being involved in the death of this righteous Person.

Not only do the apostles make no attempt to find an excuse for the behaviour of the nation, but they also refuse to take a neutral or indefinite line over it. The reality of the Holy Spirit's coming to them is made clear by their attitude to sin and wrong from Pentecost onwards. This was indeed the Spirit of light, revealing and punishing and disciplining the Church.

The message which declares sin to be sin, reprimanding those who perpetrate it, does not miss its mark. It hits the target of the human heart. None leaves the scene of this kind of preaching untouched, for it is inspired by the power and truth of the Holy Spirit. It reaches man's innermost being. It pricks his conscience, for we are told what happened after Peter's address—"they were cut to the heart" (Acts 2:37). Stephen's preaching had the same effect—"when they heard these things, they were enraged" (Acts 7:54). Life or death follows from this pricking of the heart; or, in other words, either repentance and conversion, or rebellion. When the Spirit-filled disciples uncompromisingly named the sin of their listeners, there was a decisive confrontation out of which life was born. This may be seen in the writing of Paul elsewhere: "for we are the aroma of Christ to God among those who are being saved and among those who are perishing. To the one we are the savour of death unto death; and to the other, the savour of life unto life" (2 Cor. 2:16). So too there is contrast between the reaction to Peter's preaching which provoked the question, "brethren, what shall we do?" (Acts 2:37), and that of Stephen when we read "they ground their teeth against him" (Acts 7:51).

Moreover, repentance was not the only factor involved. There was also a call to be baptised in the name of Jesus, as a member of His Body, the Church. Even this is not all, for Peter continues: "you shall receive the gift of the Holy Spirit"

(Acts 2:38). Peter plainly states that in order to receive the Holy Spirit, one must repent, believe and be baptised in the name of Jesus. Only those who are devoted to the Holy Spirit, and allow Him to work freely in them, are true members of the Church, for Peter goes on to say: "the promise is to you and your children and to all that are far off" (Acts 2:39).

How wonderful is the work of the Holy Spirit! It is He who reaches the hearts of men. He it is who causes them to repent of sin and enables them to change their attitude so that they submit to baptism in the name of Jesus for the forgiveness of sins, and so can then call Him their Lord and Saviour. But He does more than that—He gives Himself to us. If repentance and faith were all that the Holy Spirit worked in us, Peter would not have added this further promise. He widens this promise still further, for he included the children of those who believe and all who are yet "far off". It is clear that, in proclaiming this promise to believers, the apostle Peter had in mind an experience of being filled with the Spirit similar to that which he had himself received, for some time later, when the Gentiles in the home of Cornelius believed and were filled with the Spirit, he compared this with Pentecost (Acts 10:47).

It was the conviction of the apostles that individuals and groups of people who believed in Jesus were also to be filled with the Holy Spirit. For instance, in Samaria many received the message of the gospel and were baptised in the name of Jesus, but had not yet received the Holy Spirit. The apostles did not seek consolation in the thought that it had been the Holy Spirit who had caused the people of Samaria to believe in Jesus. As far as the apostles were concerned this did not mean that they had received the Holy Spirit. For it is written that John and Peter went to them and laid their hands on them that they might receive the Holy Spirit (Acts 8:14ff). It was the same later with the disciples of John the Baptist at Ephesus; they also had believed in Jesus but had answered "no" to the question "have you received the Holy Spirit?" However, after Paul had laid his hands on them, the Holy Spirit manifested Himself in prophecy and worship in other tongues (Acts 19:1-7).

Consider now the experience of Paul who, although given faith in Christ by the Holy Spirit at the time of his Damascus road conversion, did not in that same moment receive all His gifts. For the Lord ordained that Ananias a few days later should go to him, and after baptising him should lay hands on him so that he might be filled with the Spirit. Ananias also said this to him: "Brother Saul, the Lord Jesus has sent me that you might regain your sight and be filled with the Holy Spirit" (Acts 9:17). Only now could he receive his marching orders and begin to serve with authority.

The fact that those who came to believe in Jesus did not automatically receive the Holy Spirit clearly demonstrates that an experience of the fullness of the Spirit (e.g. Acts 9:17) is not necessarily given immediately, although the conversion itself is certainly brought about by the Holy Spirit. Nor does baptism by water usually include it. It is true, according to the evidence of the New Testament, that the gift of the Holy Spirit often coincided with baptism, but He seldom gives concrete gifts of the Spirit immediately. He is at work throughout the life of the believer, and He is ready to fill each one. As Acts shows, this filling of the Holy Spirit brings about something entirely new in the believer.

This is not something that happened uniquely in the lives of the apostles. But rather we see a completely new creation emerging, which did not exist before, the *ecclesia* of God. It is the creation of the Holy Spirit and formed by Him out of nothing—the New Testament Church, the Church of the saints. This new creation of the Holy Spirit did not exist when Jesus was on earth. The Holy Spirit had to come so that the "nation" of God's elect might come into being. It is certainly true that the kingdom of God was revealed in the person and work of Jesus when He was on this earth. But the New Testament Church was not born until the Holy Spirit came. Then it recognised Jesus as its Lord and Redeemer, and placed itself under His command, loving, serving and worshipping Him.

So all that Jesus had said about the kingdom of God became real not only in His Person but also in His Church. In the New Testament Church, as described to us in Acts, God's kingdom of love dawned. We are told the believers were of one heart and soul. They shared everything. Indeed we know from contemporary accounts that it was proverbially said of them: "how these Christians love one another!" In the Church, then, people who were by nature egotistical and unable to free themselves from material possessions, were completely delivered from their love of earthly goods and were able to give them away. This was brought about by the Holy Spirit, who was now filling the Church.

The kingdom of God dawned—as a kingdom of truth and light, for sin was uncovered (Acts 5) and overcome by the light. The kingdom of God was revealed as a kingdom of joy, for the Spirit of joy was poured out upon all. The joy was so great that the believers took their daily food with praise (Acts 2:47). This overflowing joy, which was a distinctive feature of the life of the disciples, shines out in this verse: "they were filled with joy and the Holy Spirit" (Acts 13:52). Even when the apostles had to suffer humiliation, they were full of joy at being allowed to suffer for the name of Jesus (Acts 5:41; 4:13). The kingdom of God was revealed as a kingdom of peace when the apostle Paul suffered in a variety of ways. He gave a compelling witness to the gospel because he did not allow his love to be embittered by his circumstances, nor did he impute evil to others. So he was a peace-maker, even for his enemies. The kingdom of God was manifested as a kingdom of power and majesty through the deeds of the apostles, empowered by the Spirit. Through them God's greatness radiated in a wonderfully majestic manner.

Thus, the ascended Lord continued, through the Holy Spirit, the work that He had begun during His days on earth—the setting up of the kingdom of God. It now became visible to the world, for there was now a group of His people submitted to the command of the *Kyrios* (the Lord). Jesus was glorified through His subjects, the believers. He was manifested as the living King, the risen Lord. Thus, the coming of the Holy Spirit made real in the Church the long-held hope of the dawn of the kingdom of God.

The activity of the Holy Spirit from Pentecost onwards is a breath-taking pageant of continuous and all-conquering power. What a mighty stir there was in the fellowship of believers! Truly the apostles had nothing in their hands, "I have no silver or gold", said Peter (Acts 3:6). They could do little to set in motion outward and organised activities. Yet there was a powerful stirring there, welling up from within and nurtured by the Spirit of God. It was something explosive, like dynamite shattering the *status quo*, and moving people to love or hatred, support or opposition. As a result strong action is seen miracles and signs were performed in the name of Jesus–"these men" it was said, "have turned the world upside down" (Acts 17:6).

A good sub-title for the Acts of the Apostles would be–"The Holy Spirit builds the Church". Always something is happening. It is all movement. Jews and Gentiles are led into dialogue and their hearts are changed as they are brought into a completely different way of life. The apostles and other witnesses for Christ are able to report remarkable things as they record the acts of the Spirit in many places. The whole missionary outreach, even as far as Europe, is set in motion at the impulse and under the direction of the Holy Spirit, resulting in the building of the kingdom of God. Every day men are saved from spiritual death and given eternal life in Christ. The believers are urged by the Holy Spirit of life and fire to pray together (Acts 4:24). Their prayer is so powerful that the place is shaken. They become importunate and cry to God for signs and wonders to be performed, and their prayer is answered. It is this kind of prayer, motivated by the Spirit, which God answers. The powerful, life-creating activity of the Holy Spirit becomes known everywhere to the God-fearing and the pagan alike. Indeed the whole of the Acts of the Apostles is full of it. It is one continuous song of praise concerning what the Holy Spirit had done.

The Holy Spirit, then, injected a stream of life into the new-born Church. We are now able to see the fulfilment of what Jesus had said to the disciples at the feast of the tabernacles: "he who believes in me, as the scripture said, 'out of his heart shall flow rivers of living water'. Now this He said about the Holy Spirit which those who had believed in Him were to receive, for as yet the Spirit had not been given, because Jesus was not yet glorified" (John 7:38,39).

But now the hour for the pouring out of the Holy Spirit had come, and the water of life was welling up in the hearts of the disciples. Ceaselessly it flowed out from them to the crowd, so that the thirsty drank, and their souls were healed as they came to faith in the Lord Jesus.

The disciples must have constantly marvelled over the miracle of the gift of the Holy Spirit, for it changed their whole life and gave them power for service. So it is understandable that Paul exhorted the Ephesian Church, which had already received the baptism of the Holy Spirit, to "be filled with the Holy Spirit" (Eph. 5:18). Those who had once tasted the glory and power for Christian living which came from receiving the Holy Spirit wanted more and more of this grace.

They wanted to be filled to overflowing. No doubt the members of the early Church thirsted for the Holy Spirit in His fullness, because they knew how desperately they needed Him.

What would the disciples have been like if the power of the Holy Spirit had not been given to them? Nonentities!—for they would not have been able to carry out any of their tasks as witnesses for Jesus. Had Ananias not laid hands upon Paul, so that he might be filled with the Spirit, Paul never could have filled a great part of the then-known world with the knowledge of the gospel. We owe to the Holy Spirit the fact that thousands in countless towns and in many lands came to believe, and that churches sprang up everywhere. It was the Spirit who urged Paul to witness about Jesus (Acts 18:5). It was He who enabled him to preach the gospel in all its power: "for the gospel came to you not only in word, but also in power and in the Holy Spirit" (1 Thess. 1:5). It was only because Paul preached the Word "in demonstration of the Spirit and power" (1 Cor. 2:4) that so many people were born again. Indeed when Festus heard Paul's witness to Jesus, he said: "Paul, you are mad" (Acts 26:24). It was the Holy Spirit who had made him so ardent. For this reason Paul urged the church at Rome to "be aglow with the Spirit" (Rom. 12:11).

The disciples were utterly dependent upon Him for their witnessing. Not only were they facing the unbelief of heathendom, but also the opposition and hatred of the religious world (at that time Jewish). Their ministry almost always included disputes, persecution, hatred, abuse and threats. Had they not been full of the Holy Spirit they

31

would have been no match for such attacks. But instead they experienced the reality of the words: "it is the Spirit of your Father speaking through you—what you are to say will be given in that hour" (Matt. 10:19,20). This comforted them and gave them the courage to withstand continuous cross-examination and persecution.

Again and again they found that they could withstand their opponents in the power of the Holy Spirit. Of the opposition they took no heed—for they said: "we cannot but speak of what we have seen and heard" (Acts 4:20). With uplifted hearts they rejoiced when persecuted by their enemies. The Holy Spirit gave them a belligerent and defiant spirit, so that they called upon the victorious name of Jesus against all the powers of hell. When Stephen spoke, he was so full of the wisdom of the Spirit that his opponents could not answer him (Acts 6:10).

The disciples had an even greater experience, for the Spirit rested upon them as the Spirit of glory when they were cruelly treated for Jesus' sake (1 Pet. 4:14). This was visibly noticeable to those who stood around Stephen, for they asserted that his face shone like that of an angel in the midst of all their abuse (Acts 6:15). Without the gift of the Holy Spirit the disciples would have remained a hopeless bunch of failures, as they had been when they forsook and denied their Master in His affliction and at His death. Moreover, Jesus had to rebuke them before His ascension for their unbelief and hardness of heart (Mark 16:14). But now, together with the rest of the Church, they were strong in the power of the Holy Spirit when confronted with suffering and persecution. The

Holy Spirit had come as Comforter exactly as Jesus had promised.

He had come as the One who glorifies Jesus in everything (John 16:14). Whether they were praying, rejoicing, witnessing—the Holy Spirit always pointed to Jesus, whom He had come to glorify. Jesus shines out in their testimonies. He shines in their faces—the crucified and risen Jesus stands in the centre. The whole work of the Holy Spirit is about Him. Through the Holy Spirit hearts are gripped with Jesus' joy, so that they surrender themselves fully to Him out of love. The Holy Spirit makes them willing to live for Christ and lose their lives for him.

The Holy Spirit had come upon the disciples as the Spirit of fire. They could do nothing else but witness to the name of Jesus, so that the people of their sinful generation might be saved and brought into blessing, even if it cost them their lives. The Holy Spirit set them on fire with the result that they were zealous for the honour of Jesus' name.

So the Church prayed for signs and wonders to be performed through the name of Jesus (Acts 4:30). The believers even asked for further signs and wonders although they had already experienced many for we are told that the people praised God for miracles of the Holy Spirit (Acts 4:21). They were consumed with a longing that God might be honoured and men's souls saved. So they entreated the Holy Spirit to reveal Himself more and more through His gifts and powers, for Jesus had promised that such signs would accompany those who believed on Him (Mark 16:17,18).

And He answered their prayer. Again and again

Acts testifies to the fact that miracles and signs were done through the apostles (Acts 2:43; 14:3, etc.). Men are freed from the tyranny of satanic powers; sick people are healed; the believers, filled with the Holy Spirit, praise God in other tongues; miracles of salvation and preservation occur; but there is also a sacrificial loss of life. It is said of Stephen that he did great wonders and signs (Acts 6:8). Philip did also. When the crowds saw the signs he performed, they gave heed to his preaching. The Holy Spirit reveals Himself in power and strength—the lame begin to leap, like the man lame from birth (Acts 5); the dead are raised (e.g. Tabitha at the word of Peter). It is as if the gates open and heaven draws near to them.

The angelic hosts are also active. The angel of the Lord appears in prison (Acts 5:19; 12:7); Stephen is given a vision of the throne of God (Acts 7:55); an angel leads Philip to the Ethiopian eunuch who is seeking God (Acts 8:26); in the midst of the danger of imminent death in a shipwreck, the angel of comfort appears to Paul and promises safety (Acts 27:23). When heaven swoops down to earth and when the Holy Spirit is at work, everything is transformed—even matter and substance. People walk through locked doors which are reported to open of their own accord. There is also the story of Philip, "caught up" to the place where he is to serve next (Acts 8:39).

The Holy Spirit also adds power and authority to prayer, so that the doors of the Philippian jail are opened (Acts 16:25,26), and men in fear of death trust God again (Acts 27:35,36). He enables men to act powerfully, so that we read, "God did extraordinary miracles by the hands of Paul"; the sick are healed and demons are cast out, even just through the touching of pieces of his clothing (Acts 19:11,12). So the acts of the disciples are carried out in the power of the Spirit according to the word of Jesus: "you shall have power from on high" (Luke 24:49). In response to this work of the Spirit new and living churches spring up everywhere—the manifestation of the kingdom of God.

4 ". . . That You Lack Nothing!"

The "kingdom of God", the "royal dominion of God", means that Jesus Christ, the Lord, is really among us. In the days when He was on earth, He spoke with authority, not like the scribes. He spoke with such great wisdom and power that even His opponents could not contradict Him. He was full of divine knowledge and was a mighty prophet, who knew what lay hidden in men's hearts. He performed signs and wonders. All the gifts and powers of the Spirit of God were joined together in Him.

If the risen Christ has complete sway in the life of His Church, then she truly represents His Body—created by the Holy Spirit. The works of the Holy Spirit will be seen in the Church, for Jesus promised that those who believe in Him will be accompanied by certain signs— signs which are performed through the gifts of the Holy Spirit (Mark 16:17,18). There are gifts of God's grace which become visible in the *charismata*, a Greek word from *charis*, which means grace, favour or kindness. With those gifts of grace God gives us all an undeserved and free gift, "which overpowers and invokes astonishment and joyful surprise."[3] The Holy Scriptures enumerate the riches of the gifts of the Spirit in 1 Corinthians 12 and 14 and in

Romans 12, viz. the gifts of wisdom and knowledge, prophecy, faith, working of miracles, healing, teaching, discerning of spirits, exhortation, help, leadership, speaking in tongues and interpretation of tongues. Taken together they transform the one Body of the Church into a living organism, and the individual members receive through the Holy Spirit different functions, which supplement each other.

What a wide range of possibilities the Holy Spirit opens up within the Church with His gifts: For He apportions "to each one individually as He wills" (1 Cor. 12:11). Usually, however, one gift of the Spirit is given to each Christian (1 Pet. 4:10). Through His creative activity the Spirit can bring into being new gifts in situations of particular need, or change them according to the need of the Church. However, the gifts of the Spirit are always given to be used in service (1 Cor. 12:7), and work together in building up the Church. Love for Jesus and one's brother are, therefore, the only possible motives for the genuine exercise of spiritual gifts, as is corroborated in the accounts in Acts.

THE GIFTS OF WISDOM AND KNOWLEDGE

We are told that when Stephen spoke, "they could not withstand the wisdom and the Spirit with which he spoke" (Acts 6:10). How much this gift meant to him when he faced such hostility! And the same was true elsewhere in the Christian Church which from the very beginning had to withstand persecution. Moreover the word of wisdom enables us "to say something which, in a given moment, hits the nail on the head, and to say

37

it in such a way as to rob the hearer of the opportunity of dodging the issue. Wisdom is in the highest sense the presence of the Spirit; it is holy quick-wittedness".[4]

In granting wisdom to His followers, the Lord gives them "a mouth and wisdom which none of your adversaries will be able to withstand or contradict" (Luke 21:15), because it is the Father's Spirit who speaks through them (Mt. 10:20). "My speech and my message were not in plausible words of wisdom but in demonstration of the Spirit and power" Paul, could say of himself (1 Cor. 2:4). Consciences were stirred, men were born again through the Holy Spirit, and many were persuaded to walk the way of the cross in sacrificial love.

What an endowment of the Spirit is this gift of wisdom! For it provides more than simply the right word for the right moment. It also unlocks the hidden wisdom of God, which cannot be grasped by human understanding alone. What the human intellect can never discover about God's thoughts and plans or about the depths of His nature, is opened up to us by the Holy Spirit through this gracious gift of wisdom. What we can never learn through the processes of rational thought or scientific reasoning, as we peer into the hidden depths and mysteries of God's being, is given to us through this gift—indeed it is put into our lap. The mighty power of the Spirit explores everything, for He is able to comprehend even the depths of the Godhead (1 Cor. 2:7-10).

The gift of wisdom permits God's thoughts about salvation to be seen in all their depth and greatness. So the Holy Spirit, through the operation of this gift, opens our eyes to God's purposes for

Israel, for the Church of Christ as a whole, for the nations, but also for local churches and individuals. Without the gift of wisdom the New Testament epistles would not have been written—(e.g. Romans 9-11) with their revelation of the plan of salvation for Israel.

The gift of wisdom again and again causes those who have received it to bow down in worship before God. For the ways of God are so marvellous and full of eternal glory that we cry out "how wonderful is thy counsel!" Through it we recognise God's wonderful guidance in situations of apparently senseless suffering, where all is dark, and human reasoning can no longer understand God. "It is the Lord who grants favours to those whom He loves" (Psa.4:3)—and we can echo the worship of the Psalmist at the thought of God's wisdom. So this gift of the Spirit, like all the rest, is given for the single purpose of leading us to worship God. So the apostle Paul breaks into praise as he thinks of God's wise ways with Israel: "O the depths of the riches and wisdom and knowledge of God!" (Rom. 11:33).

The gifts of wisdom and knowledge flow into one another. The gift of knowledge is so important and valuable to Paul that he speaks of it no less than twenty-three times in his letters. It was especially entrusted to him, for he writes: "even if I am unskilled in speaking, I am not in knowledge" (2 Cor. 11:6). Through the gift of knowledge Paul was able to serve the Church particularly as a theologian. How he had to fight against false knowledge intruding into the Church! In his zeal for sound teaching, it was never a matter of knowledge from the human stand-point or experience, nor of a legal or verbal contest. The knowledge that comes through this gift of the Holy Spirit is, like the Spirit Himself, life-giving—not a false literalism or a dead orthodoxy. We see this in the Acts of the Apostles and the epistles. The confessions of faith which have been invoked by this gift of the Spirit have down through the ages kindled love and the worship of God in countless people. It has prepared them to lay down their lives for this faith.

For Paul, then, this sound knowledge is the source of fruitfulness in the Christian's life (Col. 1:9ff.). It also enables the Christian to put others on the right path (Rom. 15:4). For him it is a matter of the Church coming to "all the riches of assured understanding and the knowledge of God's mystery" (Col. 2:2).

This knowledge, or gift of clear-sightedness, is wrought by the illumination of the Spirit, who causes us to grasp the great inter-relation of the whole of Holy Scripture, the teaching of salvation. It clarifies what is meant by redemption, justification, sanctification and by the gifts of the Spirit. Thus, the gift of knowledge is in many ways bound up with the gift of teaching, so that this divine knowledge can be dispensed to believers.

A GIFT OF PROPHECY (REVELATION AND FORETELLING)

In the first days of Christianity one revelation of the Spirit follows another. We read in Acts of the mighty deeds of God, accompanied by His revelations through the Holy Spirit. For the Holy Spirit reveals things which cannot be understood by natural reasoning. He gives Philip his instructions to go to the Ethiopian eunuch (Acts 8:29). He reveals to Paul that he is to go to Jerusalem to the Council of the apostles (Gal.2:2). He reveals to Peter through a vision, and later through a voice, that he is to go to Cornelius, "three men are looking for you . . . I have sent them" (Acts 10:19-20). He shows Paul that he is not to journey to Bithynia, and causes the man from Macedonia to appear in a vision with the request, "come and help us!" (Acts 16:7ff). In Corinth He sends a vision in which the Lord speaks to Paul and urges him to persevere; for "I have many people in this city". He says (Acts 18:9ff). In a further vision He causes Paul to hear the command of Jesus to go to the Gentiles and preach the Gospel to them (Acts 22:17ff). Paul then testifies: "the mystery was made known to me by revelation how the Gentiles are fellow heirs, members of the same body and partakers of the promise in Christ Jesus through the gospel" (Eph. 3:3,6). And in the storm at sea, the Holy Spirit gives Paul through the angel of God in a vision the assurance that he will reach home safely (Acts 27:23-24).

Thus the story of Paul's missionary journeys, and indeed all missionary activities, is that of guidance through the direct influence of the Holy Spirit. He directs down to the smallest detail what is to be done and what is to be left undone.

These revelations run through the Acts and the epistles like a scarlet thread. In the New Testament they are called *"apokalypsis"* or in other words- an unveiling. The curtain is drawn back from something which our natural mind cannot perceive. What a great gift this is! Mostly such revelations occur as visions. Whereas in the Old Testament

41

they were the experience of the great prophetic characters, according to the prophet Joel (2:28), this gift is promised to the whole Church as a sign of the new age. Peter asserts in his sermon that the new age has dawned (Acts 2:16). What was formerly just the experience of the prophets, is now God's gift to all His sons and daughters, young and old alike. It is true that there are also individuals in the New Testament Church who are called to be prophets, but they are included in the congregation and are under their scrutiny. At the same time the prophetic Spirit is at work with many revelations in many varied forms within the Church (1 Cor. 14:26).

Often a revelation through a vision includes hearing the voice of God, as Paul did at his conversion on the Damascus road: "Saul, Saul, why do you persecute me?" (Acts 9:4). And in Damascus Ananias received in a vision certain instructions. The Lord said to him through the Holy Spirit: "go for he is a chosen instrument of mine. I will show him how much he must suffer for the sake of my name" (Acts 9:15-16). It is the Spirit Himself who equipped Paul to bear witness: "for I did not receive it from man, nor was I taught it, but it came through a revelation of Jesus Christ" (Gal. 1:12).

When Paul was shown the mighty plans of God's wisdom through the gift of wisdom, he broke into adoration; so surely his heart, like that of the other apostles, would have been full of thanks and worship for this prophetic gift. Through it they experienced the direct guidance of the Holy Spirit, and knew what God's will was. For as a father talks to his son, so God talked to them through the Spirit

42

with concrete directions for particular situations when decisions had to be made.

But this was not all. At times the Lord even opened the heavens, and Paul was allowed to see into the third heaven, when God took away the veil (2 Cor. 12:1-4). What a gift this is for us, living as we do with such limitations and spiritual poverty—often knowing nothing more than we can see with our eyes! But with this gift our narrow horizons are lifted, and the divine reality breaks tangibly into the life of His people. Here we have a faint anticipation of the life in glory, where God, as He did long ago in paradise, speaks directly with us His children. Thus Jesus fulfilled His promise "I will not leave you desolate, I will come to you" (John 14:18), when He spoke to His disciples by the Holy Spirit—and this is especially true when the revelations of the Spirit were made available to the whole Church in prophecy.

When prophecy occurs in the New Testament it is, as also in the Old Testament, divinely inspired speech—so that sometimes the words of the ascended Lord are put directly into the mouth of the person who has the gift of prophecy, as in the case of Jeremiah in the Old Testament, "I have put my words into your mouth" (1:9). Such words, we are told, are "of the Son of God, who has eyes like a flame of fire, and whose feet are like burnished bronze. I know your works, your love and faith and service ... but I have this against you ..." (Rev.2:18-20).

So our risen Lord speaks powerfully to His Church, addressing her personally in this situation. There are prophetic words given to John, which he (through the gift of prophecy) has to deliver to the

43

churches of Asia Minor. In the prophetic word Jesus is really present. He is still with His people after He has ascended to heaven. He speaks in the first person through the promised Holy Spirit.

"It is probable that when John's Gospel speaks of the coming Spirit, the thought is of the Spirit manifesting Himself prophetically. He speaks in the Church almost as tangibly as the incarnate Lord Himself. The disciples are not to be left as orphans. When Jesus communicates with them from heaven through the Spirit, this will take the place of what was lost by His return to the Father. Therefore, all prophecy in the new covenant will agree inwardly with the witness of Jesus and His apostles: 'He will take what is mine and declare it to you'" (John 16:14).[5]

"The testimony of Jesus is the Spirit of prophecy" (Rev. 19:10), we are told. "Jesus wants to use the gift of prophecy through the Holy Spirit to reveal, to His Church on earth, what moves His heart (John 16:13-14). So prophecy is the expression of Christ's heart in the Church, His spiritual Body; it is the expression of His sufferings, of His joys, of His longing and of His comforting."[6]

Thus the apostle Paul exhorts the Corinthians: "earnestly desire the spiritual gifts, especially that you may prophesy" (1 Cor. 14:1), and "earnestly desire to prophesy" (1 Cor. 14:39). Paul was deeply concerned that this gift should be abundantly manifested in the Church, because "the Church is to be enlightened through prophecy in those matters which it is necessary for her to recognise."[7] The role of this gift in the New Testament churches is in keeping with this. The noun "prophet" occurs 144 times, the verb "to

44

prophesy" 28 times, and the word "prophecy" 19 times.

We are told that through Agabus a great famine was foretold to the Church, so that they were able to prepare for it (Acts 11:28), and Paul's imprisonment and afflictions were made known to him in a number of places through prophecy (Acts 20:23; 21:4, 11). Women also were endowed with this gift. When Paul entered the house of Philip the evangelist, we are told that there were four daughters of his who prophesied (Acts 21:9).

Even the writers of the Old Testament were aware of this truth: "where there is no prophecy the people cast off restraint" (Prov. 29:18). The reason for this is perhaps to be seen in the fact that prophecy includes the uncovering of sin. Jesus during His ministry on earth looked into the hearts of men and told them their secret thoughts, and continues to do so today, through the Spirit of prophecy. This was a shattering experience for the disciples in the case of Ananias and Sapphira (Acts 5:1-11). But even unbelievers are punished and judged through its operation, since the hidden things of the heart are revealed (1 Cor. 14:24-25).

The fear of God grips Christian congregations afresh. A horror of sin comes over people when they are convicted of it by the light of the truth. Such shock often leads to repentance, a change of heart, and forgiveness in Christ Jesus. For when the one who is prophesying refers to things which humanly speaking he could not have known, but which God's Spirit has revealed to him either by a vision or in words, then the judgment of God reaches men in a special way, piercing them like a two-edged sword.

What a gift this is! It is indeed a gift of grace! It frightens unbelievers and believers alike out of their indifference and laxity towards sin; it discloses hidden things, brings offences to light, causes sinners to break down. So God is revealed as the Living One and glory is given to Him. The apostle records that those who are convinced of sin through prophecy fall on their faces and worship God (1 Cor. 14:25).

Amongst the rich content of the gift of prophecy there is also revelation of the future: "write what you see, what is and what is to take place hereafter" (Rev. 1:19). John the seer is thus commissioned to pass on his revelations of the future. In addition to this powerful prophecy of the future, God has now and then raised up prophetic men in the Church, and given them the gift of seeing into the future, even if in the restricted sense of the more immediate future.

But there is yet more to this gift of prophecy–for "prophecy is not only the ability to make known the future, but the gift of seeing past, present and future with God's eyes, and making this known to others."[8] It may bring a word of warning, exhortation or a call to repentance, which contains the interpretation of God's will for the present time. Often indeed this is for the whole Church, for a nation, or even for the whole world situation. When God reveals to the prophet the stage which world history has reached, He also inspires him with a message which is relevant to it.

Because prophecy is such a sacred gift and because it has been entrusted to men in all their human weakness, the apostle Paul gives clear directions as to how to distinguish between true and false prophecy. Prophecy is to agree with Scripture. It must always be confirmed by one or two other prophets and weighed by the rest (1 Cor. 14:29; 1 Thess. 5:21). The prophet is to prophesy in proportion to his faith (Rom. 12:7). It is also his responsibility to produce nothing from his own mind, vanity or desire for power and to provide absolutely no opportunity for the spirit of Satan to enter, for it is written that the spirits of prophets are subject to the prophets (1 Cor. 14:32). Because the prophet takes part personally, his personality is not switched off in the act of prophesying, and he is responsible for what he says.

The gift of prophecy, when disciplined by the Spirit, is a mouthpiece of God of the greatest importance to His Church, for its effect often spreads far beyond the local church to the people who are reached by them. Thus where such an outpouring of this gift has taken place, congregations have again and again been filled with praise, wonder and adoration that our Lord Jesus Christ should reveal Himself through the Spirit and come so close to them.

THE GIFT OF FAITH

Over and over again God has also glorified Himself in His Church through the gift of faith. Here it is not a matter of the general kind of faith which is required of all believers, and which is fulfilled in them by the Holy Spirit. This saving faith, the very foundation of our life in Christ, is a gift beyond our understanding. But above and

47

beyond that it has pleased the Lord at times to grant to some people a special gift of faith—the faith which "removes mountains" (1 Cor. 13:2). In the epistle to the Hebrews there is a great hymn of faith which is sung about those who were endowed with faith in the Old Testament, "who through faith conquered kingdoms, enforced justice, received promises, stopped the mouths of lions, quenched raging fire" (Heb. 11:33,34). This hymn was continued in the New Testament Church through the strength of this spiritual gift. For "the Christian endowed with this spiritual gift has a supernatural capacity for seeing that God will reveal His might, justice and mercy in a particular concrete situation."[9] What opportunities the Lord gives His people to glorify His name through this *charisma!* For men with this spiritual gift experience mighty answers to prayer for the sake of the kingdom of God. They are enabled to withstand the superior forces such as human opposition, insoluble problems, worries and tasks which would otherwise lead to a break-down. This gift imparts great powers of faith, and strengthens us to hold on to the promises of God. The effects of this faith which "removes mountains" are just as great. Thus some men are called through their works of faith to be a sign to others that God is alive and performs miracles today. Through their gift they glorify the God who answers prayer, keeps promises, is yea and amen, and who is able to do all things through His almighty power.

This gift of faith edifies the Church in times of opposition, impossible circumstances and persecution. The triumphant progress of the Gospel, which was the experience of the apostle Paul, was based on this kind of unshakable faith. When God's followers tread these ways of faith, He is greatly praised and the faith of others is strengthened. Many are brought to a loving trust in the Father. What an evangelistic potential there is in this gift of faith! For through its operation many can be brought to faith in God, and believers can be led into new faith and action.

THE GIFT OF WORKING OF MIRACLES

Through the operation of this gift Jesus fulfilled the promise He had made that certain signs would follow those who believed in Him: "In my name they will cast out demons . . . if they drink any deadly thing, it will not hurt them." This was Paul's own experience at Malta when he was bitten by a poisonous viper and remained unharmed (Acts 28:5). Miracles were already in evidence when Moses caused the plagues to come upon Egypt. In the New Testament it is said of the two witnesses between the sixth and seventh trumpet calls: "if anyone would harm them, fire pours from their mouth and consumes their foes; if anyone would harm them, thus is he doomed to be killed. They have power to shut the skies that no rain may fall in the days of their prophesying, and they have power over the waters to turn them into blood, and to smite the earth with every plague, as often as they desire" (Rev. 11:5,6).

But miracles are chiefly seen in warfare against demonic powers. The crowd was amazed at the signs and wonders which Jesus performed. As evidence of their discipleship Jesus commanded His followers to cast out demons (to exorcise)

49

(Matt. 10:1), and at His ascension He reaffirmed this particular sign (Mark 16:17). In Acts we see the realisation of this, as the apostles cast out demons (Acts 16:18; 19:12). In this ministry the all-conquering power of Jesus Christ is manifested, so that satanic powers have to retreat whenever His name is invoked with the authority of the Spirit.

THE GIFT OF HEALING

In a similar manner, tremendous things happened in the power of the Spirit when this further gift was manifested in the power of the name of Jesus, for He had said: "they will lay hands on the sick and they will recover" (Mark 16:18). Just as healing was characteristic of the earthly ministry of Jesus, so it was also with the apostles and disciples, for the Saviour handed on this ministry to those who formed His Body, the Church. In addition, therefore, He guaranteed to them the authority to heal the sick (Matt. 10:1, 8; Luke 9:1, 2).

So the New Testament is woven through with accounts of numerous healings, which serve to reflect God's glory more and more. Not only did the man who was healed "leap and praise God", but, we read "all the people saw him walking and praising God" (Acts 3:8,9). Indeed people who were eye-witnesses of the working of the Spirit in healing turned to the Lord (Acts 9:35).

People are freshly challenged by Jesus the Saviour whenever there are healings. The presence of the living Christ, who said "I am the resurrection and the life", can be felt. Cures, which are effected in the name of Jesus, reveal to people that the stream of divine life is continually flowing from the One who is Life. His strength is given not only to revive soul and spirit, but also to heal the bodies of sick people and to awaken new life.

In contrast, we are shown in the New Testament that Paul did not miraculously heal his helper Epaphroditus, who was near to death (Phil 2:25ff), and he left Trophimus ill at Miletus (2 Tim. 4:20). He recommended a natural remedy to Timothy for his stomach trouble (1 Tim. 5:23), and he himself had to suffer his "thorn in the flesh" (2 Cor.12:7).

Thus the New Testament Church shows us that Christ can be glorified both through a genuine miracle of healing and through patience in suffering which is willingly borne out of love for God. One can never say that faith in Christ can in every case bring about healing, or that sickness is in every case a consequence of personal sin or a sign of unbelief, or that we should not make use of the skill of doctors or the healing properties of medicine. Our heavenly Father has Himself designed these for our help. "Honour a physician" we are told, "with the honour due unto him for the uses which you may have of him: for the Lord has created him. For of the most High comes healing . . . The Lord has created medicines out of the earth, and he that is wise will not abhor them" (Eccles. 38:1ff).

But what a great blessing it is that the Lord has also given us the gift of healing through the Holy Spirit. Ought we not as children of the Father to make use of it to His glory?

THE GIFT OF TEACHING

The gifts of the Spirit were given to build up the Church—and to bring in Christ's kingdom in the world. The Spirit effected the authoritativeness of the witness, and teaching was a necessary stone in the building, in order that the Church might become the temple of the Holy Spirit. The addresses of Peter and Paul are evidence of this genuine and authoritative teaching. What do they teach? Paul wrote that he knew nothing except Jesus Christ and Him crucified (1 Cor. 2:2). They teach the truth that Jesus Christ is our redemption and sanctification, our wisdom and righteousness. They teach the truth that nobody comes to the Father except through Him. They teach about the love of God and His salvation and the consequence of His sovereignty. They teach about things to come, of the last days and the Antichrist. They teach about the return of Christ, the Last Judgment and the setting up of the final kingdom of Christ, when every knee shall bow to Him. They teach about the glory of heaven, and what our transformation will be like.

The letters of the New Testament are evidence of this Spirit-activated teaching. They show that this teaching can never be detached from life, but is always a result of the life which has its source in the Holy Spirit alone, a life of repentance, love, discipleship and sanctification.

What a difference between the spiritual gift of teaching and all human teaching! For charismatic teaching allows the Holy Spirit and not human wisdom to be seen. In this the Spirit-inspired teaching is closely linked with the gifts of wisdom and knowledge. It is inspired by the Word of God, for it is the gift of expressing in a convincing way the treasures of God's Word and our dependence on it in practical living. In the early Christian congregations, through the Holy Spirit's influence hearts were opened to the teaching of the Word, which was living and lucid, and they received the Bread of Life. Through this gift they received God's word when it was expounded to them. This gift was so precious to the early Church that we are told "they devoted themselves to the apostles' teaching" (Acts 2:42). Indeed Paul can boast that the Corinthian church was "enriched by Him, in all teaching and in all knowledge" (1 Cor. 1:5). (The word "teaching" in this verse is from the German translation of the Greek word *logos*; it is translated "utterance" in the AV and "speech" in the RSV.)

Because true teaching is a gift of the Holy Spirit, true teachers are specially commissioned for their ministry. God has "appointed" them (1 Cor. 12:28). They are then, called by God to this particular office. Because of this, James warns: "Let not many of you become teachers . . . for you know that we who teach shall be judged with greater strictness" (James 3:1). For teachers can lead large numbers of people either to life or damnation. What is taught is believed and forms a basis for life. Teachers who have followed the precepts of Jesus will be great in the kingdom of heaven. Those who have taught that His commandments should be kept "shall shine like the brightness of the firmament; and those who turn many to righteousness, like the stars for ever and ever" (Dan. 12:3). Conversely, those who falsify the teaching of Jesus, taking away from the standards of God's holiness and His laws, are small in the kingdom of heaven (Matt. 5:19). Indeed they will be judged in terms of James 3:1. The danger that such false teaching might intrude was great, even in the times of the apostles. For example, it was taught that sin need not be taken seriously, because it was already cancelled for sinners through the atoning death of Jesus (Rom. 3:7,8; 6:1). Or that the New Testament Church need no longer fear the wrath of God, but could practise worldliness (Eph. 5:6), or that Jesus never required people to deny themselves for His sake. Thus the offence of the Cross was avoided, and it was no longer taught that the way of the Cross was the only one befitting to a Christian, for Jesus had said "whosoever does not bear his own Cross and come after me, cannot be my disciple." But, if Christians were no longer to follow the way of the Cross, they would no longer be "in Christ", they would merely be a misrepresentation for Jesus. They would fall away from God, disgrace the Lord, and bring perdition and destruction upon themselves (Phil. 3:18,19).

Because false teaching leads the life of a believer down the wrong road and so to damnation, the apostle warns us very earnestly, "if anyone teaches otherwise and does not agree with the sound words of our Lord Jesus Christ and the teaching which accords with godliness, he is puffed up with conceit, he knows nothing; he has a morbid craving for controversy and for disputes about words . . ." (1 Tim. 6:3,4). The New Testament Church knew that only those who received the true teaching and lived according to it, could be blessed in the Lord and inherit God's glory.

So we see that, then as well as today, there was a battle for sound teaching against false teachers who were perhaps even leaders in the churches. "From among your own selves will arise men speaking perverse things to draw away the disciples after them" (Acts 20:20). Again and again the direction comes "to take note" of the teaching (Rom. 16:17). And with strong words the apostles warn against heretics, whose lives correspond to their false teaching, who live for themselves and their desires (2 Peter 2; 2 Tim. 3). The apostles took very seriously the danger of such false teachers in the Church, because they knew the catastrophic consequences of their influence, ruining life and gambling away salvation itself. As John says: "if anyone comes to you and does not bring this doctrine (Christ as truly God and man), do not receive him into the house or give him any greeting" (2 John 10).

Those to whom has been given the office of a teacher bear a very heavy responsibility in those days as well as today. They need the *charisma* of teaching as well as the inspiration of the Holy Spirit so that they can say with the apostles, "we impart this in words not taught by human wisdom but taught by the Spirit" (1 Cor. 2:13).

THE GIFT OF DISCERNING SPIRITS

The life of the Church was endangered not only by false teaching, but also through the misuse of spiritual gifts. We are told of lying prophets and false apostles. The gift of discerning of spirits was, therefore, crucially needed by the Church. It enables men to discern those who were, "holding the form of religion but denying the power of it" (2 Tim 3:5). This gift helps us to make spiritual diagnoses, to penetrate to the root of motives and to distinguish clearly between what is godly and what is human or diabolical.

One of the bitter complaints of leaders of the New Testament Church was that wolves in sheep's clothing were intruding, at the same time confusing and laying waste the Church because their diabolical agency was not recognised, and they were able to disguise themselves by their pious language as angels of light (2 Cor. 11:13-15). This was the reason why they were not opposed. So they were free to draw the congregation imperceptibly with them to final destruction.

Those who had been empowered by the Spirit had to step into this confused situation with the gift of discernment: as we see in Paul's letters once when "filled with the Spirit" he described the false prophet, Bar-Jesus, as a "son of the devil" (Acts 13:9-10). At Philippi Paul does not allow himself to be blinded by the apparently spiritually perceptive words of the fortune-teller. He exposes the demon and orders him out (Acts 16:17,18).

Through the operation of this gift, the apostles were able to discern not only the significant spiritual trends and the entry of hypocrisy into the Church, but also the working of the Holy Spirit in the manifestation of His various gifts. By means of this check, Paul recognised that the words of the woman at Philippi were not prophecy but divination. Paul knew that every spiritual gift of God could be imitated by the enemy, as he apes Jesus Christ in devilish forms of caricature and distortion. John also warns his readers, "do not believe every spirit, but test the spirits to see whether they are of God" (1 John 4:1).

The gift of discerning spirits not only reveals the satanic, but also indicates the extent to which spiritual gifts are derived purely from the Spirit of God, or whether they have been adulterated by something from within man. Paul demonstrated this gift, for instance, when the disciples in Tyre apparently told him "through the Spirit" that he was not to go to Jerusalem (Acts 21:4). He did not follow their counsel, for it was not the instructions themselves but only the knowledge of the danger which was from the Spirit, as was confirmed by the prophecy of Agabus, who enacted the Apostle's arrest with his girdle (Acts 21:11).

The apostle Paul recognises the fact that self can be mixed in with spiritual gifts through vanity and the desire to dominate. It is for this reason that he exhorts the Thessalonians to test prophecies. But he does not say that prophecies are no longer to be made because something from the human mind always obtrudes. On the contrary he exhorts the Thessalonians: "do not despise prophesying" (1 Thess. 5:19-21).

Paul proved the truth of the saying "the spiritual man judges all things" (1 Cor. 2:15)—he seems to have a right judgment in every kind of situation—while the person who lacks this gift and is not filled with the Spirit, goes astray in his judgments. He cannot distinguish between what is of the flesh and what is of the Spirit, because he himself lives according to the flesh. So the gift of discerning spirits was of the greatest help to the New Testament Church, which from its very beginnings had been tempted by various spirits and powers and at the same time it contained the dangers of carnality.

The object of the activity of the Spirit in the operation of these gifts is that Christians minister to one another in love. That is why the gift of exhortation was regarded so highly by Paul. As a result of this he addressed this urgent request to Timothy, "I charge you in the presence of God and of Christ Jesus . . . convince, rebuke, and exhort, be unfailing in patience and teaching" (2 Tim. 6:1,2). Also he urges the Roman Christians to exercise this gift—"he who exhorts, in his exhortation" (Rom. 12:8).

Paul himself took very seriously this ministry of exhortation. "Working together with Him then", he writes, "we entreat you not to accept the grace of God in vain" (2 Cor. 6:1). He calls all evil clearly by its name—"I appeal to you, brethren, that all of you agree and that there be no dissensions among you" (1 Cor. 1:10). Or again, "I entreat Euodias, and I entreat Syntyche to agree in the Lord" (Phil. 4:2). Encouragement was always included with exhortation. Even when Paul writes to the Thessalonians to exclude a stubborn sinner from the assembly, he nevertheless adds that they should treat him as a brother (2 Thess. 3:15). Paul's admonition stems from a fatherly love, and he can say of himself: "for you know how, like a father with his children, we exhorted each one of you and encouraged you and charged you to lead a life worthy of God . . ." (1 Thess. 2:11,12).

Paul knew how to comfort and exhort others, because he himself had lived through many conflicts and sorrows, and had experienced in them "the Father of mercies and God of all comfort" as well as the Father who chastens. Paul writes to the Corinthians about the God "who comforts us in all our afflictions, so that we may be able to comfort those who are in any affliction, with the comfort with which we ourselves are comforted by God" (2 Cor. 1:3,4). Paul himself was a sinner who had previously persecuted the Church. He had received the gift of forgiveness, and could bring to others the comfort of Christ's forgiveness of sin. He had himself been through innumerable sufferings, and so could also comfort others who had had to endure affliction with the same comfort which had comforted him.

This gift of exhortation and pastoral ministry will be given only to those who have had the experience of the comfort of God's forgiveness, for they have trusted in the Father's love and received forgiveness and the cleansing of their sins. Only those who have had a personal experience of God's holiness and wrath, and are horrified at the sin from which they have been redeemed through Christ's forgiveness, can practise the ministry of admonition. They take sin seriously, and have the courage to tell them the truth in counselling, to face their enquirers squarely with the horror of their sin, and to bring them to repentance in the power of the Spirit.

This *charisma* of caring for souls involves both love and understanding of the other person as well as a merciful but uncompromising calling of sin by its name—as well as a call to forsake it. This is a spiritual gift of utmost importance to the ministry of the Church.

If the apostles were to witness, that is present the kingdom of God in the power of the Holy Spirit and operation of His gifts, then there was a need also for this gift. Indeed, its importance was so great that they appointed special deacons, who were called by the Holy Spirit to this ministry. The story is told in Acts 6 of these Spirit-filled men, who gave this kind of ministry to the Church. They met the need which had arisen in a constant spirit of sacrificial love (Rom. 12:7). God also appointed special "helpers" in the New Testament Church (1 Cor. 12:28), who had the important task of lending a hand where it was necessary.

Such helpers performed acts of love under the direction of the Holy Spirit, who enabled them always to intervene at the right moment and in the right way. At the same time they were given an authoritative word for those whom they assisted in practical ways and through gifts. For instance, there was Phoebe, of whom Paul said in praise, "she has been a helper of many and of myself as well" (Rom. 16:2). Exercising charity, that is giving away part of one's property, should take place under the guidance of the Holy Spirit: "he who giveth, let him do it with simplicity", Paul writes (Rom 12:8 A.V. See also 1 Cor. 13:3a). All this takes place in the Church in the name of Jesus – for Him and for the brethren in all simplicity – that is without expecting either acknowledgement or reward. For those who are endowed with this gift of mercy and service this verse is particularly apposite: "blessed are the merciful, for they shall obtain mercy" (Matt. 5:7).

Just as the human body with all its various functions must have direction, so it is necessary for the members of the Church with their different gifts. Even if in the last analysis it is Christ Himself who is the head of the Church, He has given us on the earthly level various offices. The members must, therefore, be under the control of a leader who is appointed to direct the congregation. For this reason some are called to the office of leader (Rom. 12:8; 1 Cor. 12:28). Peter speaks of shepherds of the flock (1 Pet. 5); Paul, of bishops (1 Tim. 3; Titus 1); and he exhorts them: "take heed to yourselves and to all the flock, in which the Holy Spirit has made you guardians, to feed the Church of the Lord" (Acts 20:28).

The gift of leadership is the gracious gift of the Spirit for this office. The Greek word for it (*kybernysis*) means the art of helmsmanship. This spiritual gift enables men to lead large or small groups of people, for it is the leaders and shepherds who are responsible for the final directions. The leader must be able, like a helmsman, to steer the ship of his congregation between all the rocks and shoals to the ultimate goal—the city of God. He takes care that the Church remains in a living relationship with Christ, the Head, that it is nourished through sound teaching from the Word of life, and that its love for Jesus remains alive and the way of discipleship is not forsaken. He continually encourages the church in its ministry of mutual help and edification. So he sees to it that all the gifts of the Spirit are rightly administered and that life in the Church blossoms under the leadership of the Spirit.

Together with the office of leadership, God gives Spirit-filled men an aptitude for pastoral care, making them like the "great Shepherd" (1 Pet. 5:4), who led His flock so wisely, lovingly and humbly. Therefore, Peter also says of the shepherds that they are not to be domineering "over those in your charge" (1 Pet. 5:3). Jesus, our good Shepherd, was among us, as He says, "as one who serves" (Luke 22:27).

Where there is leadership, therefore, as given by the Holy Spirit, there is never dictatorship, but full freedom for the whole organism of the Church to function with its spiritual gifts; and yet there is a leader there who has responsibility for the flock and who is inspired by Jesus and His Spirit. There must be such leaders, directors and shepherds in the churches, for where these divine offices have been despised, the consequence has been disorder and disunity. There has been opportunity for false teaching, and charismatic movements have developed wrongly. The leader of a church or fellowship must oppose every manifestation of spiritual error, disorder or evil, even if he incurs enmity through it, as, for instance, we read of in the letters in the Revelation of John (Rev.2:2,9).

How important then is Spirit-filled leadership! An example of this is the Council of Jerusalem. At that time it was touch and go whether there would be schism between Jewish and Gentile Christians. Only the spiritual presence of mind of the apostle James brought them to the unanimous decision of which it is said, "for it seemed good to the Holy Spirit and to us" (Acts 15:28). But on the other hand, whenever the office of leadership is no longer exercised as a gift of the Spirit, but is used instead in human organisation and for the quest for power, the results have always been disastrous.

Because the Holy Spirit wants to raise up a living Church, the very embodiment of the principle of love, office and *charisma* must be properly related. Individuals were often given a special office which they practised within the orderly framework of congregational life. On the other hand the exercise of the office needed the Spirit's authorisation and consummation through bearers of gifts. Unfortunately office and *charisma* have tended to develop separately throughout the course of church history, and this has raised many questions and difficulties. How wonderful it is when they are united in Spirit-filled leadership and pastoral care! (Eph. 4:11). Such people bring decisive influence to bear upon the Church. Great responsibility rests on their shoulders. For this reason Paul requires that honour should be given to them (1 Tim. 5:17), and urges, "those who labour among you and are over you in the Lord ... esteem very highly in love because of their work" (1 Thess. 5:12,13).

THE GIFT OF SPEAKING IN TONGUES

This gift unlike the previous ones, was given, not so much for ministry to people, as to God Himself. Jesus says of it, "in my name they will speak with new tongues" (Mark 16.17). It is true that Paul had to warn against the over-valuation of this gift, when it was being over-emphasised through human vanity and conceit, rather than being used in God's glory. Yet he also writes, "I thank God that I speak in tongues more than you all" (1 Cor. 14:18). Indeed this gift of the Spirit does enrich the Christian's prayer life. When the Holy Spirit prays in other languages within us, it becomes evident that we are the temple of the Holy Spirit. He bears witness to Himself that He is in us by praying in languages which our intellects cannot manufacture. So this spiritual gift consists in the reproduction of an actual language. "The Greek work *glossa* in 1 Cor. 14 has clearly the sense of 'languages' Glossolalia presents a miracle of speech and language, a miracle of words, a liturgical miracle which must be seen in its relationship to the miracle of Pentecost."[10]

The apostles and others at Pentecost, and later the groups which received the Holy Spirit, spoke in new languages. The evidence of the coming of the Holy Spirit on the fellowship in Cornelius' house was that they began to speak in new tongues. Peter says that they had received the Holy Spirit exactly as the disciples had at Pentecost (Acts 10:47). It is to be assumed that for the most part glossolalia was given as a matter of course with the outpouring of the Holy Spirit upon congregations.

To this gift belongs also "singing in the Spirit" (1 Cor. 14:15), which together with "praying in the Spirit" had a special place in the early church and enriched its worship. "The heavenly Word was the source of this *charisma* also, as all liturgy on earth is an echo of the heavenly liturgy . . . glossolalia was both inspired word and inspired music. The glossolalic speech was often uplifted rhythmically and melodiously sung. To this extent glossolalia presents an early form of sung liturgy in church music."[11] Through this worship in the

Spirit—praying and singing, God was worshipped and glorified.

Because the gift of the Spirit called "the interpretation of tongues" was usually present also in the Church, everyone had a part to play in the praying and singing which the Holy Spirit was inspiring in the believers. This "interpretation", another gift of the Spirit, is brought directly to the person without the interpreter having the least idea of what the spiritual language is. The words of the interpretation are, therefore, a revelation, either to the original speaker in tongues (1 Cor. 14:5, 13), or, more often, to another (1 Cor. 12:10, 30: 14:2b). The directness and spontaneity of such prayer which is disclosed through interpretation, is a living message to the congregation.

But there is yet more to the gift of tongues. "He who speaks in tongues", Paul writes, "edifies himself" (1 Cor. 14:4). In other words—he brings himself into a relationship with the divine source of life and consolidates this relationship. He develops it, and receives from the depths of the Godhead a progressive renewal and spiritual remoulding of his being. He surrenders himself to the powers of the age to come, "he gives himself up to the Son of God as his Lord, and is filled with the blessings of sonship."[1 2] Indeed in this praying and singing in tongues Paul says we are uttering "mysteries in the Spirit" (1 Cor. 14:2). Thus the whole being is taken up in worship into the presence of God, and the apostle says, not without reason, "now I want you all to speak in tongues" (1 Cor. 14:15).

5 Spiritual Gifts—
Burden and Blessing

These gifts of the Holy Spirit were certainly a boon and blessing to the New Testament Church, but at the same time they were a burden and brought suffering. For wherever God's Spirit is working there is opposition, persecution and abuse. The enemy's territory is invaded and souls are snatched from his clutches. He is, therefore, on his guard, otherwise great victories are won for the kingdom of God and he suffers heavy losses.

So the enemy fights with his sharpest weapons, and his tactics are always the same. For instance, Stephen is accused, "we have heard him speak blasphemous words against God" (Acts 6:11). They said the same about our Lord Jesus when He drove out the demons in the power of the Holy Spirit. It is also said of Jesus, "it was out of envy that they had delivered Him up" (Matt. 27:18). In the case of Stephen it was the jealousy of the religious people which provoked their attack upon him. So we see that the causes of the abuse and persecution of the Church are the same as they had been for Jesus. Religious people who lack the power of the Holy Spirit often persecute those who have His authority. The experience of people like Stephen, Peter, John, Paul and other disciples, reveal that those who are empowered by the Spirit share the fellowship of His sufferings. "Nothing so leads to affliction, in the train of the slain Lamb, than the possession of the *charismata*. Their possessors are abused and disowned, secretly glorified, banned and burnt by their contemporaries, yet held in honour by later generations."[13]

Those endowed with spiritual gifts arouse opposition when they declare with prophetic insight God's will for their contemporaries, which includes exhortations and warnings. There are many references to this in the Scriptures. Because sin is uncovered through such men, and the glory and power of God revealed, they are hated, persecuted and ill-treated like the prophets of every age. But greater than the worst persecution, even martyrdom itself, are the accompaniments of the Spirit's gifts—the opened heavens and the divine glory, for instance, witnessed by Stephen. If we view the other spiritual gifts, such as healing, faith, tongues or the working of miracles, we notice that blessing was not the only accompaniment. We are also told of the trouble which resulted from them in the lives of the apostles. Paul, who possessed the gift of healing, was himself not healed and sought God in earnest and repeated prayer (2 Cor. 12:7, 9). It must too have cost him something to leave Trophimus behind seriously ill (2 Tim. 4:20). Only in those circles where the gifts and powers of the Holy Spirit are accepted is disappointment great if the gift does not bring the expected results. This is part of the suffering of those who are gifted by the Spirit. The responsibility for the right use of the gift rests heavily upon those to whom it has been entrusted. This means that again and again they have to come to a point of surrendering their wills to God, so that He is able to use the gift as He pleases.

Also Paul often experienced the withdrawal of the power to work miracles, which God had given to him, when faced with particular cases of need. Often he was not rescued but knocked down and stoned. He was storm-tossed for days on the sea. It is true that he had the gift of faith, and through it an unusually clear certainty in his heart of the wonderful leading of the Lord, as when he was assured of the safety of the sailors, because of him, in a most terrible storm. But we do not know whether or not this was the result of agonising struggles and temptations. Everyone who has the spiritual gift of faith has to tread a dark pathway, where at first there is no answer and where faith is continuously difficult until help finally comes.

Only the daring stand to lose. Only those who expect much can be disappointed, but they will never be disappointed by God. This applies particularly to the hazardous venture of the apostles and disciples when they surrendered to the Holy Spirit and allowed themselves to be endowed with gifts and so become His instruments. They had the courage to enter upon this adventure of faith. In doing this they discovered that God did not allow them to fail in their times of temptation. For example, when Paul experienced the great disappointment of not being healed, he received through this experience a greater gift of the Holy Spirit. He learned that it was in weakness that God's power was perfected in him, and he was able to bear witness to this in the churches that he founded (2 Cor. 12:9).

If prophetic utterance and the working of

miracles brought testing and persecution to the apostles, they experienced similar invective and slander when they spoke in tongues. This also, like every gift of the Spirit causes division. Because speaking in tongues, being a miracle of language, was so incomprehensible, those who had this gift were scorned by those who were unable to understand it by human reasoning. It was offensive to them that the new language given by the Holy Spirit eluded control by our human faculties. The day of Pentecost was not the only occasion for scorn and sneering. The verdict of those who heard the glossolalia of the disciples may well have spread like wildfire through Jerusalem and the nation, "they are filled with new wine" (Acts 2:13).

The gift of tongues was not confined to the original disciples, but was given beyond the confines of Jerusalem. In Samaria, for instance, where Simon "saw" that the Holy Spirit was given after apostolic laying-on of hands (Acts 8:18), in Caesarea (Acts 10:46), in Ephesus and in Corinth. We can deduce from Paul's account (1 Cor. 14:22,23) that the believers here also experienced misunderstanding and mockery. As church meetings were also evangelistic, since they attracted many Jews and Gentiles, strangers to the faith would have heard glossolalia, and as the apostle Paul says of himself that he spoke in tongues more than them all (1 Cor. 14:8), he may also have prayed in tongues at meetings where an interpreter was present. In doing so he may perhaps have been subjected to mockery also.

One sees also in this gift the conflict between flesh and Spirit, for the carnally minded understand nothing about the Spirit of God, and thus approach the things of God with human perception and understanding. Because they cannot understand them, they fight against them. Speaking in tongues as given by the Spirit is contrary to all rational thinking, even that of a believer. So reason rebels against it. For such people it is a "foolish" gift, and human wisdom revolts against it, making itself out to be wiser than the God who created it. So people will say: "If praying in tongues has to be interpreted, why cannot the prayer be in comprehensible speech in the first place?" In saying this, people fail to grasp the unique possibility of expressing the inexpressible as is given in the gift of tongues. The interpretation is not always a translation, but often an indication of the content of that which is beyond our power to express. Such an indication is, however, quite clear in its message.

Paul's repeated teaching about "the foolishness of God" (1 Cor. 1:25), is applicable to the gift of tongues also. It is precisely that which man cannot reason out, but which comes from the Spirit Himself, which contains the greatest wisdom, for "mysteries of God" is used as a description of this gift (1 Cor. 14:2). Because of this Paul exhorts. "do not forbid speaking in tongues" (1 Cor. 14:39).

So also the gift of discerning of spirits is not only an incomparable help and guide, but carried with it a heavy burden of responsibility. For Jesus says in the letter to the angel of the Church in Ephesus, "you have tested those who call themselves apostles and are not, and found them to be false" (Rev. 2:2). Thus this gift makes us responsible for exposing hypocrites and those who corrupt the Church. Wherever this task is carried out, there comes division in the Church, for the apostle Paul writes that those who "hold the form of religion but deny the power of it" are to be avoided (2 Tim. 3:5). Thus men with this gift must call people to separate themselves from others, and so bring about splits in the church for the sake of the truth of Christ. They must have the courage to appear to be bringing unrest and distress into the church. They will be hated and persecuted by those who are exposed, and from then on avoided because of this; for these people, because they have a dishonest character, will seek their revenge.

But even when the gift to discern spirits leads to straightforward brotherly admonition, it is still burdensome. For example when Paul used his gift of discerning spirits to see through to the inner motive, he could not refrain from opposing Peter relentlessly (Gal. 2:16). What a risk he was taking for he was only the least of the apostles while Peter was a pillar of the Church! In doing this, Paul risked losing Peter's love and respect, as well as that of most of the believers. But he acted according to the principle he himself asserted, "am I seeking the favour of men, or of God? If I were still pleasing men, I should not be a servant of Christ" (Gal. 1:10).

In spite of all the sufferings which spiritual gifts brought them, the disciples who had experienced Pentecost, and the apostle Paul, held the Holy Spirit and His gifts sacred, and did not allow themselves to be confused or led astray in controversy or opposition. With reference to the coming of the Holy Spirit, Jesus had said to them before His departure, "you know Him" (John

14:17). Now they were allowed to know and experience Him, the Paraclete, the Comforter, power from on high. How could they drive such a regal guest from their lives? Their Master had said to them that He would be in them, and remain with them for ever—so the Holy Spirit with His gifts was a holy bequest to them, and they were ready to bear even suffering and shame for His sake.

6 *The Secret of Those Empowered by The Spirit—Repentance and Love*

The gifts of the Spirit cannot be used correctly if they are removed from a particular fertile soil. They must be bedded in. Or to put it another way—they must be interwoven with a particular type of behaviour and manner of life. This is very important and needs to be stressed because there are some groups in which the gifts of the Spirit are used independently of the behaviour of those who manifest them. However, the apostles teach us differently in Acts and the Epistles and, if one changes the emphasis there, one is forsaking the biblical foundation.

We need to examine the biblical mode of conduct, and the gifts must not be separated from it. We need to discover the attitude underlying the use of His gifts by those whom the Holy Spirit has blessed and empowered. Peter once wept bitterly over his denial of Jesus; Paul experienced a deep repentance for his great sin of persecuting the Church of God. Thus the infilling of the Spirit and the bestowal of spiritual gifts were received on the basis of a penitent heart. The first part of the message of the preacher to the people was, therefore, "repent" (Acts 2:38). When churches and people received the gifts of the Spirit, the apostles knew they could only be correctly

73

manifested on the basis of a penitent heart. We also
see from Paul's letters that one single act of
repentance was not enough to ensure that the
infilling of the Spirit and the distribution of
spiritual gifts would be fruitful. This penitent
attitude of heart needed to be lifelong. So Paul
regarded himself from his conversion onwards as
"the foremost of sinners" (1 Tim. 1:16). Many
years after this event he still writes that he is not
worthy to be an apostle because he has persecuted
the Church of God. (1 Cor. 15:9).

The evidence that a congregation or individual
Christian is living in a state of repentance is that sin
is taken seriously. But the basis of this is a life lived
in the context of the holiness of God. Witness to
this may be found in Acts and the New Testament
epistles. Sin was exposed again and again, and as a
result repentance was repeatedly given and resulted
in a new dimension of spiritual life. So the apostle
Paul could write: "for godly grief produces a
repentance which leads to salvation and brings no
regret" (2 Cor. 7:10). Because the church could
only survive where this happened, sin was
relentlessly exposed and dealt with.

According to the Spirit there is no difference
between the action of Moses in his righteous anger
against sin when the golden calf was set up, and the
zeal of Paul against sin and sinners in the Church of
Christ. So, in the same letter in which he deals with
spiritual gifts, he enquires whether they ought not
to mourn over sin so that the sinner might be
removed from among them (1 Cor. 5:2). Indeed he
says that this man is to be delivered to Satan for
the destruction of the flesh.

He further demands that they should have no

dealings with undisciplined people in the congregation who bear the name of brother for the sake of appearances, nor immoral persons, idolaters, slanderers, drunkards or robbers. They were not even to eat with such people (1 Cor. 5:11,12). Again he demands, "drive out the wicked person from among you" (1 Cor. 5:13). To the Thessalonian church he writes that the members should withdraw themselves from every brother who lives a disorderly life, and does not govern himself according to Paul's instructions, "note that man, and have nothing to do with him, that he may be ashamed. Do not look on him as an enemy but warn him as a brother" (2 Thess. 3:14,15).

The Acts and the epistles show us that in the early Christian churches whatever sin or weakness developed, one thing happened—they "walked in the light" (1 John 1:7). This means that the sin was brought to the light and the sinner disciplined. Indeed even the leaders of the church made a point of standing together in the light of God. As already mentioned, the apostle Paul openly challenged Peter in the assembly for deviating from a sound proclamation of the way of salvation (Gal. 2:14). And the apostle Peter allowed himself to be corrected. There was no hang-over of bitterness, for his letter expresses much love and appreciation of Paul.

So the Church stands in the light of God. And the spiritual gifts are to be handled in this holy context. Whatever it was that came by the inspiration of the Holy Spirit, whether it be revelations, prophecies, miracles, healings, powerful prayer, or words of wisdom and knowledge, this was the pre-requisite of their genuine practice.

Certainly they were received by sinful men. But mostly by those who were submitted to divine discipline, who stood firmly in His light, who lived humbly in the congregation and so were continually renewing their repentance. And where this did not happen, as in Corinth, the apostle had to intervene with righteous zeal. In the epistles very little is said about the gifts of the Spirit, probably because they were rightly used in the way described above.

The foundation for the exercise of spiritual gifts lay in this matter of repentance and daily walking in the light and presence of a holy God. So, as we see in Acts, it was possible for the kingdom of God to be built up by the gifts and powers of the Holy Spirit, and indeed for the foundation to be laid for its entire history over the next two thousand years.

If then we are longing to see the Spirit and power of God demonstrated in our Christian service, above all we must walk in the light. This means that we must surrender to the holiness of God, allowing ourselves to be corrected and chastised by the hand of God and the admonition of men. Through this we are led again and again to repentance and self-abasement, and learn how to be delivered from sin. As Jesus put it, "if your eye causes you to sin, pluck it out and throw it away." Then the foundation will be sound for a true unfolding of spiritual gifts. But wherever, in church or fellowship, this congregational discipline is not continuously exercised, wherever sin, small and great, even the spirit of judging others, is not continually brought to the light, we no longer stand on biblical ground. So, according to biblical teaching, the message of the authority of the Spirit and His gifts should not be given without also stress being expressly and continually laid on walking in the light and on repentance.

The Acts of the Apostles which supplies us with information about how we may experience demonstrations of spiritual power, not only reveals to us as a background penitent men who take their sin seriously, but also those who, in their consuming love for people, sacrifice themselves for Jesus, and this also gives us an understanding of the gifts and their effect. It is within the context of this life of sacrifice that spiritual gifts are to be seen.

Paul is insulted, abused, thrown out of synagogues and cities, and beaten. He is outlawed, despised and rejected. Again and again they seek his life, and this is especially true of his Jewish bretheren, to whom, in spite of this, he belongs. But he has only one answer—love. Indeed he would happily give his life so that even a few of them might be saved. He is never tired of loving and suffering. He keeps on entering synagogues, and seeking out his brothers. Despite his later emphasis on his mission to the Gentiles, he nevertheless persists in his approach to his Jewish brethren.

It must have been even more painful for Paul when he was misunderstood and slandered by the churches whose spiritual father he was. Indeed he found out that people were even working against him. Paul's reply to these endless injuries is in fact an even greater miracle and witness to Jesus Christ than the miraculous acts and gifts with which the apostle had been endowed. He says in 1 Cor. 4, "when reviled, we bless; when persecuted, we endure; when slandered, we try to conciliate; we have become, and are now, as the refuse of the world, the offscouring of all things."

This reveals overwhelming love like that of our Lord Jesus Christ, whose glorious love was most strongly seen in the midst of unspeakable sufferings. The picture painted for us in the New Testament is of constant, forgiving and sacrificial love. This love is the mainspring of the believers' actions and their Spirit-filled achievement, even involving physical suffering, as Paul says in 1 Cor. 4:11, 12, "to the present hour we hunger and thirst, we are ill-clad and buffeted and homeless, and we labor, working with our hands."

Paul graphically describes his sacrificial life in 2 Cor. 6 and 11; it involved much irksome work, countless imprisonments, many beatings, danger of death, and five scourgings. Once he was stoned and another time flogged. So he handed over his body to suffering and yet worked on and made the great journeys during which he was shipwrecked three times. His work involved him in many strenuous and dangerous journeys by foot; he suffered sleepless nights and deprivations, hardship and troubles, cold and want.

We can now understand why God was able to provide Paul's mighty ministry with exceptional evidence of the power of the Spirit. In him the ground was prepared for the Spirit's work to take root and flourish. On this altar the flame of sacrifice could blaze up and set many on fire.

Without such a background the Holy Spirit could not have worked in this way through the apostles. Only along this path did the gifts of grace move effectively. So Paul found it necessary to speak about the way of love in the midst of the discourses on the gifts in 1 Corinthians 12-14—a love which includes all the gifts of grace, and yet is greater than them all, "I will show you a still more excellent way" (12:31). Here Paul describes Christ's way, along which he has travelled, the way of sacrificial love which is not self-seeking, but subordinate to that of others. This love includes our enemies within its scope. It does not impute evil, or become embittered. It does not keep a tally of other people's faults. It forgives all things; hopes all things for others, and is patient in every circumstance.

When the lord allows the way of love to radiate its beauty through Paul's writings, in the midst of a catalogue of spiritual gifts, he is teaching that spiritual gifts will be correctly used when they are all saturated with love. Let them spring up from the fertile soil of the love of Christ! In 1 Corinthians 13, Christ's character and way of life shine forth in all their beauty and glory, and before them all the gifts lose their lustre. Only what is born of this love demonstrates the majesty of God and will bear fruit. The correct operation of the gifts can only spring from love, otherwise something spurious results, for what the Spirit imparts is affected by the condition of heart of the believer.

So when the Holy Spirit comes to us and wants to endow us with His gifts, He plainly requires of us that we adopt the pattern of love. In 1 Corinthians 14 this is described as "making love your aim". It is not a gift of grace with which we are suddenly and unconditionally endowed, but an attitude of character, and, therefore, all the more precious. This will, however, only remain ours by means of the battle of faith, the Spirit against the flesh, of which Paul writes, "for the desires of the flesh are against the Spirit, and the desires of the Spirit against the flesh; for these are opposed to each other, to prevent you from doing what you would. But if you are led by the Spirit . . ." (Gal. 5:17,18a).

Our flesh, as our old Adam, seeks to give anything but love. The apostle describes in 1 Corinthians 13 our true nature. We seek our own advantage, we allow ourselves to become embittered, and we impute evil. We are egotistical and inconsiderate. It is therefore the duty of one who strives after spiritual gifts and manifests them to carry on this battle relentlessly on the principle of love and against his own ego. He must trust in the redeeming power of Jesus Christ, and in the activity of the Holy Spirit, who wants to transform us into the image of Jesus.

So we come again to the same conclusion: only men who really call sin sin, and look the sin of lovelessness straight in the face, and who begin to hate this sin and wage war against it to the bitter end, only these have the right demeanour for spiritual gifts. But where this battle is not fought the believer will allow himself, often without noticing it, to be controlled by his "fleshly nature", which argues, judges and slanders, gives in to impulses, and is full of envy, jealousy, bitterness and self-seeking. And then all gifts, whether faith, prophecy, sacrifice, or speaking in tongues are, as the apostle puts it, "nothing" (1 Cor. 13:2).

Is it possible for us to work for the kingdom of God in the power of the Spirit if we leave no room for Him, or if we resist His work against our self-centredness? It is the same Spirit who gives the gifts and who also transforms our characters. So it is impossible to say: "I have the Holy Spirit and His gifts", and at the same time to reject Him when He does His work of transformation. For in so doing we lose His gifts and powers, or we find them so overgrown with our own self-centredness that the Holy Spirit cannot effect His real aim of glorifying God.

This challenge and conviction concerning sin, through the operation of the Holy Spirit, is not, however, a once-for-all experience at the time of conversion or before we are endowed with the gifts of the Spirit. Rather the Holy Spirit has a life's work to accomplish in us. He must continually challenge us freshly, as we again and again fall into sin, often without noticing it. He must constantly remind us, rebuke us and chasten us. This difficult transforming work of His, which He carries on tirelessly in our souls, is greater than all the gifts which He lavishly distributes.

The one who does not resist the Holy Spirit in this area, but rather allows the work of transformation to be effected in Him, experiences an authority crucially different from that received by a less mature Christian through the gifts of the Spirit. The one who has been thus purified has an authority which is the product of a state of character. It is clear that this likeness to God gives us the greatest authority—greater than that of the spiritual gifts.

So we meet, among mature Christians, men who are sanctified and transformed into the image of Christ. They speak words of peace and love. Their every word is wise, regardless of the special gift of

81

the word of wisdom. Through their close
relationship to the Lord, the wisdom of His
salvation is opened up to them. It is evident that
God has given them perception and they are able
to witness to others about their knowledge of God.
Their encouragement to others is an authoritative
pastoral ministry. Their words are strong to
comfort or exhort. They have faith to believe that
the Lord can do everything. In the inner harmony
of their life with Christ they perform powerful
miracles. Because love for Jesus is paramount in
them, the Spirit having worked a transformation,
they are eager to worship. Indeed, when Jesus has
taken control of a man and shaped his life, more or
less everything that he says and does is Spirit-filled
and powerful.

Such people bring forth richly the fruit of the
Spirit as it is called in the Scriptures (Gal. 5:22;
Eph. 5:9). Thus the fruit of the Spirit is different
from the gifts of the Spirit. Its pre-conditions are
different. The fruit is produced over long periods
of preparation, for fruit can only appear when a
particular process has been gone through. The
death of the grain of wheat is the essential
pre-requisite for growth and ripening through
storm and sunshine.

This takes place in people who have allowed
themselves to be chastened by the Spirit and
corrected in God's way, who have accepted the
Father's loving discipline as true children. They
have continually fought the battle between flesh
and Spirit, and won, so that the image of God
might be formed in them. The tireless activity of
the Holy Spirit in the soul is manifested in the
Spirit-dominated character; it allows Him to shine

forth as the Spirit who is transforming it and who never tires in His work until the soul mirrors the image of God.

We cannot fully comprehend the activity of the Holy Spirit. He bestows gifts on men who have only just received Jesus as their Saviour. His work continues ceaselessly in their souls. He transforms them little by little into the image of Christ and regulates the use of the gifts according to their proper inner attitude. He equips us with gifts and powers, but at the same time He takes care that we do not deal with them as with something that is at our disposal and operate them independently of our own personality. Rather He sees to it, as Acts shows, that we are continually repenting and battling against sin. He makes us ardent in our search for love and commissions us as people authorised by Jesus Christ on the basis of a new attitude of life, the attitude of love. All this we owe to the one Holy Spirit who endows and blesses us with gifts; who leads and admonishes and convicts; who disciplines us, and fights in us against the flesh, and prays and intercedes in us. He is the Spirit who gives us life, and who continually delivers us from our dying condition and helps us in our prayer life. When we realize who the Holy Spirit is and what He does, we can only stand in awe, worshipping, adoring and praising Him.

7 *The Holy Spirit in Church History*

The Church of Jesus Christ, as Acts shows us, was built through the activity of the Holy Spirit, through His powers and gifts. The Word of God tells us that the gifts of the Spirit are irreplaceable and necessary for authority, today as in those days.

Christian living, which is "in demonstration of the Spirit and power", gives an authority to our work for Christ, and it is this which the good Shepherd is eager to bestow. This equipment is as essential now as it was then, for the life of the Church, in its warfare against the spiritual powers of evil. With it the Head gives His members power to withstand many forms of temptation. Today He provides them with the gift of discerning spirits, wherever new and misleading spiritual movements influence the Church from within and without. Today He gives them the gifts of faith and working miracles especially in view of the threat of nuclear war. If there are today the evident signs of the rise of the power of the Antichrist, the Lord through the gift of prophecy is giving the Church the right word to arouse and prepare it for this situation.

The early Church, which was called into life in a most extraordinary manner through the creative power of the Holy Spirit, needed the gifts of the Spirit for its edification. How much more do we need them today when our church is so often lifeless. People are relying on their traditions and customs, or are exploring the Scriptures in the power of human intellect. But only the Holy Spirit can lead us into deeper understanding.

But this Spirit does not manifest Himself apart from His gracious gifts. They are not meant to be replaced by pious human effort in understanding and receiving the Word of God. The Spirit alone can enlighten, prick the conscience, and lead to repentance, submissiveness and reconciliation. Only the Spirit can create understanding of the signs of the times and lead people to stand in the breach as the end of the world draws near.

None of this will take place through the reciting of formal creeds, or through prayer groups or conscientious private prayer which is merely the result of our human activity and energy. Without the Holy Spirit such action is dead. Only the life-giving Spirit can prepare the Church for the coming of the Lord. Only where He gives Himself with His gifts can the Church be given the impetus to make inroads into the world's darkness.

Therefore everyone who is concerned that God should be glorified before the eyes of unbelievers and is concerned that many people should be won for Him through the working of the Holy Spirit will strive for the gifts of the Spirit. Whoever prays and intercedes that the churches may become alive at this time of climax in the war against darkness and death, prays that the Holy Spirit may come down afresh and bestow gifts of grace. For even, where the spiritual gifts are already available in a church, Paul still cries out, "be filled with the Spirit" (Eph. 5:18). How much more would He ask of us who have such a paucity of gifts! If every command in Scripture is mandatory, how can we exclude the command to seek for gifts?

But have there not been churches which had no spiritual gifts and yet were full of life? This we must counter with the question: do we know for certain that such spiritual gifts were not available in these churches, including speaking in tongues? The spiritual gifts may not have been particularly evident. This, however, does not exclude the possibility. Could a living church really lack Spirit-induced testimony and calls to repentance, spiritual gifts of wisdom and understanding, Spirit-authorised pastoral ministry and healing (which often happens secretly), right up to the worship and glorification of God through faith? It is always through the agency of the Spirit of God together with His gifts that a live congregation is so stirred that God the Father and the Son are praised. So the Spirit spreads God's greatness abroad and makes visible the power of Christ's redemption.

It is our Lord Jesus Himself who wants us to ask the Father to send us the Holy Spirit (Luke 11:13). As before Christ's ascension everything depended upon the disciples' having Jesus, so for His Church from His ascension to His return, everything depends upon our receiving the Holy Spirit after we have believed in the Lord Jesus. In this context it should also be said that Jesus urges His followers to knock at the Father's door with their request for the Holy Spirit like the friend in the parable (Luke 11:5-8). For Jesus wants to indicate to us in this parable that when we want to receive this altogether precious gift we must ask

George Muller's work of faith is an equally fine testimony, for he supported 2000 orphan children without ever appealing for money. He received support only through prayer and his faith in God. God was greatly praised through this gift of faith. Indeed countless people have been encouraged by his faith to tread a similar pathway through which God has yet again been glorified.

The founder of the China Inland Mission, Hudson Taylor, who had the gift of faith, is known to have confessed that when he set out for London, as a first step towards missionary work in China, he had only a few pounds in his pocket but otherwise "nothing more and nothing less than all the promises of God." His faith was not disappointed. God kept all His promises. In the history of this work, God who is "yea and amen", the Almighty, who performs miracles, was again manifested to the world. Men were led to faith and God was given the glory. So it happened that a missionary fellowship, still young, for it was scarcely twenty years old, in no way underwritten financially and facing the greatest difficulties, was challenged by such tremendous tasks that it had to have new workers. One of the missionaries proclaimed his goal of faith: one hundred new workers in the next year. At first Taylor shared the general opinion that this was asking too much. A hundred new workers in one year when the staff as a whole had not yet reached two hundred!

However, when he was able to have a few days of quiet and prayer, the Spirit of faith suddenly came upon him. While he was dictating the letter home, he could only say "we are praying for and expecting a hundred new missionaries to come out in 1887." His eager faith so flamed up that he said to his secretary, "if you showed me a photograph of the whole hundred, taken in China, I could not be more sure than I am now."

And this year 1887, introduced by two days of prayer, actually ended with the last batch of the "hundred" sailing for China; all the work could be carried out, all expenses were paid and great blessing extended over a wide circle.

In this dimension of faith God not only displays His greatness, but also His fatherly love, for He hears the cries of His children and gives men courage to pray. For the gift of faith is always linked with the gift of prayer. Men who have the spiritual gift must wrestle in prayer with almighty God as Jacob did. They are completely and solely dependent upon Him, so that they live in the flame of His holiness. So they are continually blessed and judged by God. They are above all His true children. As children they must always beg for everything. But at the same time as children they experience the Father's love for them, and they have the privilege of abiding in Him.

If through the gift of faith God is glorified as Father, so, through the gift of performing miracles, the victorious power of Jesus is revealed. Through this gift the name of Jesus has already been glorified before thousands. When Johann Christoph Blumhardt spoke the authoritative word "Jesus is Victor" and so broke the power of Satan over Gottliebin Dittus after two terrible years of conflict, it became known far and wide. A human soul had been freed from the severest form of demonic possession, and was able throughout her later life to live to God's glory as a witness to the redeeming power of Christ.

Blumhardt was through the Spirit's power then able to help many more find the way to peace and light, whether insane, spiritually deranged or tired of life. The work of the Spirit through him inspired also innumerable people to cry out in their need or temptation, or in struggles with the powers of darkness—"Jesus is Victor". Jesus, the Conqueror, the Lamb of God who has broken the power of the enemy is glorified through this spiritual gift. And not only Blumhardt, but many whose names are not known, have through this gift brought about the miracle whereby satanic forces have been broken, and spirits of darkness made to yield. Souls freed from the bondage of the enemy have been captured for Jesus. So right up to the present time there have been those who like Paul have "worked miracles among you" (Gal. 3:5).

Missionaries have also experienced the literal fulfilment of the promises of Jesus concerning the working of miracles. He said "if they drink any deadly thing, it will not hurt them". The missionary Nommensen working in 1860 in Sumatra was served with food which was so poisoned that when his dog ate some of it he died immediately. His enemies, who assumed that he would die, found him alive, and were so overcome by this miraculous sign and his love for his enemies which caused him to forgive them, that they became open to the message of the Gospel.[17]

Jesus is also glorified today and revives the Church through the gift of healing. Jesus used to heal to show that the power and works of the devil were destroyed and His kingdom had come. "He went about doing good, and healing all that were

91

oppressed by the devil" (Acts 10:38b). It is still the same today. Wherever healing takes place there the kingdom of Jesus is revealed. Jesus is seen to be the Lord to whom power has been given over body, soul and spirit, and who performs miracles of healing to this day. Johann Christoph Blumhardt is a good example of this also. When he had won the battle with demonic powers in his congregation, there followed a movement of repentance and revival by the Holy Spirit. Blumhardt was not only able to help many to inner release after confession of their sins, but also through the laying-on of hands and prayer, many physical healings took place. Hunchbacks were straightened, cripples were able to walk again, eye troubles, tuberculosis and bone diseases disappeared. In all this the presence of God was so strongly experienced that eye-witnesses later said of these events, "At that time miracles and the experience that Jesus was really there belonged to the usual course of events. The presence of the Lord was so tangible that the miraculous was looked upon as the natural thing and we made no fuss about it." However, the members of the congregation continually came together with thankful hearts to offer their praise for such blessings.[18]

This gift of blessing is promised to believers (Mark 16:17,18) and especially to the elders of the church. They should always pray over the sick (James 5:14) because every sick person in the congregation should really be brought to Jesus. He said: "Come unto me all who labour and are heavy laden"—and this includes the sick. So it should be natural, as is sometimes the case in Anglican and

Episcopal churches, to add a short service of healing to church worship. At this service either the minister walks down the pews pronouncing a blessing and words of Christ's forgiveness over the sick people or the sick come to the communion rail.

God can also be glorified today through the gift of wisdom. In so many lands Christians are persecuted, having to defend themselves and endure agonising interrogation. What a gift! The right answer is given them so that their opponents cannot gainsay it, or God's Spirit causes His Word to be such a weapon in their hands that all attacks of the authorities must come to nought (Matt. - 10:17-20). This gift has already been experienced in Chinese prisons where men have their human personality systematically destroyed in a devilish way.

Dr. Leslie Milan, the founder of the Freedom Movement in Canada, describes his experiences during rigorous imprisonment in China where he had to undergo the torments of this brain-washing. "The Communists were able to wash out everything from my memory. No education was available any more, no kind of cultural background to form any resistance. Nothing of my own could resist any more. My body could not resist, for it broke down completely after several weeks. I was a physical wreck. There was nothing in me that could offer resistance. But when God's Spirit wanted to bring something to mind, out of the subconscious, *He* could still do so. As soon as God's Spirit recalled the Word of God to my memory, my tormentors no longer knew what to do. I can still hear how they challenged me and

93

said, Mr. Milan, stand up and answer this question!" They asked me—and I don't even know what it was they asked me. I could no longer even listen. Suddenly God's Word began to flow in me and when they had finished their talk and allowed me to speak, all that I did was simply to 'quote' what was in me—God's words. And these seven men of the political indoctrination course sensed for a moment something of the glory of God. It was a witness to them of how powerfully God's Word works through the Spirit . . ."

The gifts of the Spirit are still at work in many different ways today and are all gifts of the one Holy Spirit—the holy activity of the triune God, for the Holy Spirit proceeds from the Father and the Son also, who have sent and commissioned Him to bestow the gifts. So inevitably the gifts must be holy and valuable to us—particularly since Jesus specially commended the One who bestows the gifts as His own substitute when He left the world.

We must, therefore, only measure the gifts against Holy Scripture—what it says of them, and the esteem which it gives to them. We are not to measure them by their misuse, which has frequently occurred—as for instance in false prophecy and the misuse of speaking in tongues. If we do this we shall be deviating from the Bible. When Scripture says—"earnestly desire the spiritual gifts" (1 Cor. 14:1), we can never turn around and say "keep clear of the spiritual gifts", or "oppose them because there have been false prophets with spurious predictions, perhaps satanically induced." We are only to fight against their misuse, never against the gifts themselves.

The gift of prophecy in particular is of special value to us today. For truly the Chruch without it is like a parched field. "Prophecy continually brings into the life of the church a breath of divine freshness and directness. Through it there is a continual stream of new life being breathed into the words of Scripture, without which it is a dead letter. The existence or non-existence of the church depends on whether there is prophecy within it."[19]

We need prophets today—men who speak to our generation as God commands. We need men who see what lies behind the trends of our day, for instance in politics. Prophetic words spoken with authority must call the Church to follow the true way. They must cause the light of the Scriptures to penetrate everything that obscures and camouflages issues. We need them also to fulfil the missionary task, for in revealing sin and bringing hidden things to light, they bring men to their need for forgiveness from Jesus. They help to bring about decisive conversions.

Prophecy today reveals also important things about the immediate future, as well as divinely interpreting past and present events. In 1855 an eleven-year-old peasant boy in Armenia began to write down prophecies of a Turkish invasion. The Christians were warned that they would be killed if they did not emigrate to a land beyond the seas. The maps and sketches which the boy drew after he had seen his visions were recognised to be America. In 1900, now a man, he spoke again of his prophecies and pressed his friends to leave Armenia. On the strength of this the revival fellowship to which he belonged emigrated to the

United States. In 1912 the last of these families left Armenia and in 1914 the first world war broke out. The Turks conquered Armenia and three million Armenians were killed. Thus God can use this gift of prophecy even today for the protection of His people.[20]

The gift of prophecy must be prayed for, since the Holy Spirit instructs us to ask for gifts. Otherwise we can fall prey to mystification, false teaching and demoniac trends. Nothing should hinder us from praying for this gift, certainly not the fact that there have been many false prophets. It was so in the Old Testament as well as the New, and it is so in our times. Although Paul experienced misuse in his churches, he still exhorts them "not to despise prophesying" (1 Thess. 5:20).

Men with the genuine gift of prophecy are a necessity today. We have far too few. Jesus encourages us to ask the Father to give us the Holy Spirit, and the apostle Paul exhorts us twice, "earnestly desire the spiritual gifts, especially that you might prophesy" (1 Cor. 14:1, 39). Who is there who harkens to this call? Who is there who finds himself compelled by the challenge from the Scriptures, and has prayed for it with the earnestness of the friend who knocked continually because he was in such need? The bread he asked for was essential to him (Luke 11:5ff). It is just as necessary in our day for us to receive spiritual gifts, and the gift of prophecy has first place among those we should beg for.

What an awakening there could be in the Church today if what is amiss could be made clear by the lightning stroke of prophecy! Outsiders would even today, as the apostle says, fall down on their faces

(1 Cor. 14:25)! They would see themselves unmasked in their sinfulness, and would honour God, who searches and knows the depths of the human heart.

Something akin to this gift of prophecy, revealing as it does the human heart, was given to the well-known Cure d'Ars, who saw through the most pious of masks, and openly told those who came to him for pastoral care what their sins were. A simple peasant priest, unlearned and outwardly homely, he was full of self-sacrificing love, childlike humility, and led a rich prayer life. Using the authority in the Holy Spirit, he brought about such blessing that the people streamed to him in crowds. The stage-coaches from Lyons put on special services. The pilgrims came from all walks of life. They had one thing in common—they came as sinners, that is, as people who knew more or less clearly that there was something wrong with their lives. Here, however, they experienced the penetrating exposure of their sins and this in turn brought them face to face with God's holiness and resulted in many cases of decisive conversion. Indeed it led them through their encounter with Jesus Christ to a new life.

What a responsibility! God offers His people this gift, but on condition that they ask for it. In many cases we fail to ask and so do not receive it. So we are guilty of the souls we fail to point to Jesus because we lack it. For God not only uses the exposition of the Word, but all the various gifts that the Word promises, so that He might be glorified, His Church edified and outsiders brought to faith.

So we must receive this gift of the Holy Spirit.

What damage we do when we despise such a gift, and do not stretch out our hands for it! For in prophecy we experience the living Jesus, who speaks to us here and now. He addresses us in a holy and loving manner. We recognise Him as the triumphant Lord in the midst of His Church. In a particularly direct manner He makes Himself known by the imparting of spiritual gifts. Dead orthodoxy and humanly inspired belief are cut across. He is there! A word which is so personally directed to us from Him is hard to avoid. It usually brings more people to conversion than general preaching.

The prophecies and revelations of Sadhu Sundar Singh also contributed in this way. He writes about them: "when I stood up from this time of prayer I saw a shining Being standing before me, clothed in light and beauty. He spoke not a word. Radiant beams of life-giving love streamed from Him with such power that it penetrated right into my soul and flooded it. Immediately I knew that my dear Saviour was standing before me. I jumped at once from the rock on which I had been sitting and fell at His feet . . .In those few seconds He filled my heart so full and spoke such wonderful words that even if I wrote many books, I could not possibly tell it all. For these heavenly things can only be expressed·in a heavenly language. Earthly tongues are inadequate. Nevertheless, I shall try to write down a few of them which came to me through this spiritual vision of the Master." In another place the Sadhu writes, "in Kotgarh fourteen years ago, while I was praying, my eyes were opened to the heavenly vision. Everything looked so alive to me that I thought I must have died and my soul had entered into the glory of heaven; but in succeeding years also these visions have further enriched my life. I cannot cause them to come at will, but usually when I pray or recollect, sometimes eight or ten times in a month my spiritual eyes are opened . . ."[21]

Many people have been challenged by Sadhu Sundar Singh's visions of heaven and his words of prophecy over the seriousness of eternity, and have been awakened and converted. How much the revelations of men like Jung-Stilling, Pastor Oberlin and Michael Hahn, and their insight into the world beyond, have been a help to men's souls! Let us thank God for this gift of grace, whereby in our time as well as that of the apostle Paul he still occasionally draws back the curtain and allows us such glimpses into heaven that we are eager to reach the goal.

Not just one, but all the gifts of the Spirit must be in operation today in the Church of Christ. This applies even to the gift of speaking in tongues. Indeed, the Holy Spirit, who is the same today, will not allow a gift to lapse which even Jesus designated as one of the signs following those who believed in Him—namely, speaking in other tongues. It is this gift which gives us the words to worship when our own words fail because the glory and love are too great for our human speech to find words to express them. Then it is that the Holy Spirit, "intercedes for us with sighs too deep for words" (Rom.8:26). He who alone can plumb the depths of the Godhead gives us the words to worship the Almighty, holy and eternal God, whose nature we can never discover. He worships in us in these new languages given by the Spirit.

So the Holy Spirit, who works independently of how busy or tired we may be, helps us in this perpetual prayer. This means much to us, as we live in an age in which we are always busy and in a rush—threatening as it does to suffocate all spiritual life. The Holy Spirit worships in us without our help or even our intention to worship at the time. In this way also He intercedes through us and leads us to pray relevantly for this or that person, for He knows the need of the moment. He lends a hand in our weakness and powerlessness, when we are all too often unaware of the detailed need of a person, church or commitment. He knows what we need to pray for most, and His prayer has authority. He also wrestles in us when we pray for those who are tormented by the powers of darkness. This is especially helpful for the times we are living in, in which there is great darkness.

The gift of tongues helps us not only in intercession, but also is particularly useful when we are being tempted. The preacher David Wilkerson has experienced this in a definite way in his work among the drug-addicts in New York City. Many of them were wonderfully freed from severe drug addiction, when from a medical point of view they virtually had no chance. When one of these youths, relapsed again, in spite of every possible support while he underwent voluntary treatment by withdrawal, Wilkerson asked himself what it was in the other boys which led them to successful release. From one after the other he heard the story of their recovery, and what gave them the power to resist. They spoke of the reality of the Holy Spirit which they had experienced in their lives and particularly the gift of praying in tongues; when the Holy Spirit prayed in them they could resist the otherwise superhuman temptation.[22]

An account of the Indonesian revival shows another way in which the Holy Spirit uses praying in tongues. At the annual mission conference of the Indonesian Missionary Fellowship, the Spirit of God quite clearly showed the Indonesian brethren, through the agency of a missionary address, their responsibilities for the peoples of South-East Asia and North Africa. The leader of the fellowship, however, resisted this world-wide task on the grounds that many areas of Indonesia were not yet reached with the Gospel. When he laid this question before God late that night in private prayer, he was led in the Spirit over the countries of South-East Asia. It was a unique experience. He had a bird's-eye view of these countries, whereupon a burden of prayer for these districts was given him to an unexpected degree, and he began to pray for them in a language which he did not know. He felt that it was one of the languages of those countries. This action of the Holy Spirit shook the mission out of its parochial outlook, and since then it has been preparing to send out the first Indonesian missionaries to Cambodia and Thailand.[23]

This special grace of prayer which the Holy Spirit confers with the gift of tongues ought to be available to the whole congregation through the gift of interpretation. For through it prayer fellowship is enlivened in the way that so many prayer groups long for. Through this gift of interpretation the whole meeting is gripped by God's presence—by the Spirit's words and revelation, and touched by a heavenly reality. In this way the gift can help to bring the Church to life today as has happened again and again. "In truth we see, if we are acquainted with the real history of the early Christian Church, that speaking in tongues was by no means a curiosity, but rather, in all great revivals, a consistent phenomenon. When the Holy Spirit takes possession of the whole man, then both the conscious and the unconscious mind must be permeated."[2][4]

There is another gift of the Spirit which is very important to us today, as we enter upon a new age—I believe we are entering the last days—of an age of confusion of spirits. It is the gift of discerning spirits. Whoever does not have this gift, or does not belong to a congregation whose leaders have it, is in danger of falling prey to heresy. In this gift the word of Jesus becomes particularly relevant for our day—when in His kindness and concern for us He said, "I will not leave you desolate, I will come to you," He has come to us in the Holy Spirit and still wants to come today so that we may not be given over to seducers, but may know how to distinguish with the help of the Holy Spirit between those messengers who are appointed by God, and seducers and hypocrites.

We hear today so many views expressed in books and magazines calling upon us to forsake words like "God", "sin", "repentance" and "grace" out of love for our fellows. One must show understanding to people for whom God is dead. They say that this is real love. On the Christian side we are called upon to show indulgent understanding to those who live sinfully. Homosexuality, adultery, and so on are clearly labelled "sin" in the Bible. We are told, today, not only to tolerate them, but also to accept them because of their unusual character, even to the point of denying the existence of sin, because the coming of Jesus has disposed of sin and it can no longer be imputed. Large numbers of people accept this form of argument because they have become blind to the truth and have allowed themselves to be led into error.

So we need men today who are equipped with the gift of discerning spirits. They must relentlessly expose the true motives lying behind man's refusal to recognise God: his failure to proclaim Christ's redemption and victorious resurrection, and his refusal to call sin by its proper name. It·is Satan who is at the back of all this. He has only one aim, that sin may be given free rein, and that men may be ignorant of God's judgment of wrath upon sin because it is no longer preached. Thus sin is no longer evaluated as sin, and men fall more and more under the destructive power of Satan.

In view of such devilish powers of temptation, the normal spiritual experience of the Christian is not always adequate for discerning seducers, heretics, and hypocrites from those who are the true leaders of the Church of Christ. More than ever this is proving inadequate in the last days, for which there are specific prophecies about deceiving spirits in disguise, and we already have had some experience of this in our own day. Only through the gift of discerning spirits is it possible for such spirits to be unmasked in the sight of the church. Just as the leaders and members of churches and spiritual movements live under this threat of deception, so also spiritual gifts are today in danger, as they always have been. This is precisely the Church's present predicament, namely that the gifts can be satanically imitated. We know of healings at the present time, proclaimed in the name of the Trinity, which are under occult control. We know of glossolalia in heathen nations or under occult satanic influence. We know that prophecy corresponds to soothsaying, and the gift of the word of knowledge with clairvoyance. So the Church is called to test and measure everything—"every spirit which confesses that Jesus Christ has come in the flesh is of God, and every spirit which does not confess Jesus, is not of God. This is the spirit of Antichrist" (1 John 4:2,3).

So we can hold on to the clear guide lines of the Scriptures, given to us to assess rightly the spiritual gifts. For example, we recognise divine prophecy, as we do all the gifts of the Spirit, because it agrees with the total witness of Holy Scripture and does not go beyond it. Let us, however, beware of prophecies from spiritually impure sources, "new revelations" which do not do this. They are often piously dressed up human wish-fulfilment, dreams or longing for power. Such "new revelations", accepted as absolute truths, have repeatedly led to the formation of sects, and in the past decades their influence has greatly increased. We can, then, accept everything which is consistent with the Scripture, and which brings about repentance, reformation, and peace with one another, as genuine divine prophecy. Demonic prophecies, on the other hand, make people full of fear and restlessness, and bring divisions. They are not self-consistent. They are full of contradictions and often consist of empty phrases or wild apocalyptic pictures.

Where the Holy Spirit is really at work imparting spiritual gifts, it will be just like the early days of the Church. There will be no unbridled ecstatic behaviour produced by hysteria or an evil spirit. All gifts that come from the Spirit of God are manifested quietly and with dignity under God's control (1 Cor. 14:33,40). They do not attempt to draw attention or to cause a sensation. For Jesus says, "by their fruits you shall know them", the nature of those who are endowed with genuine spiritual gifts is always humble and characterised by love and a readiness to serve. The gifts of the Spirit benefit simple and humble work, while demonic inspiration results in a breaking down of these.

Paul's statement, "test everything. Hold fast to that which is good" (1 Thess. 5:21), has a modern application. For the normal spiritual awareness of the Christian is inadequate in some borderline cases to distinguish between the gifts of the Spirit and their spiritual adulterations or diabolical perversion. On the other hand, without the gift of discernment, it will repeatedly happen that true gifts of the Spirit will be said to have been diabolically inspired, as happened centuries ago.

Many who loved Jesus fell under the inquisition of the exceptionally pious, who did not know that they were fighting against the Holy Spirit and His gifts. So the gift of discernment of spirits is necessary today not only to reveal the misuse of spiritual gifts, but also to, "recognise as such the true bearers of God's gifts and not erroneously to condemn them as diabolically inspired."[2][5]

In all this confusion, amidst all the need and deadness of the Church, it is imperative that we earnestly bring to God this daily petition, like the man who knocks at his friend's door to ask for bread—"Give to members of the Church the power to discern spirits! Give us the gifts of the Spirit today!"

8 *Testimonies from the Sisterhood*

THE GIFT OF FAITH

The Father had given us a piece of unobtainable land, little "Canaan," the land of promise.[26] But it did not have the appearance of a "promised land" for it was waterless, parched and dusty due to its light, sandy soil. Through the particuarly hot summer of that year even the stretches of grass were burnt up; the vegetable plots were dried up and there was no evidence of fruitfulness and abundance.

Our pleas and supplications for a spring or at least a well were laughed at by the experts: "Geologically speaking one of the most unfavourable places for finding water here in the Rhine valley." But through the gift of faith we had the firm assurance that God would produce water miraculously. He would make this land green and fruitful. Still nothing happened. We continued to pray. We had learned in the meantime that the Father often links His answers with inner stipulations. So we longed for nothing so much as a new spirit of repentance. Were not these connected—hearts without tears of repentance and a land without springs of water? A long time went by. Canaan was landscaped, and we built the bed of a lake. The town had provided some old cobble-stones for it, and a firm had donated the cement. We had no shade; the sun beat down relentlessly and the whole land longed for water. For weeks hardly a drop of rain had fallen. Interested visitors at the edge of the future lake asked the Sisters who were building it where the water was to come from . . .

Without the gift of faith to support us, we Sisters would have stopped such a senseless enterprise at this point. Indeed, most of us would never have begun it. But faith does not run away, nor can it draw back.

We do not know what the workmen thought when we circled the bore-holes several times a day with songs of faith and victory as the Israelites circled the fortress of Jericho. But we do know what an expert in such matters said in front of the assembled congregation during the Festival of Thanksgiving for Water in the Herald Chapel: "That water has been found on this land is not a miracle. Everywhere at some depth or other ground-water will eventually be reached. But in this district I have already had over a hundred wells bored. In comparison with them the yield of this well on Canaan is twenty to twenty-five times as great as in any other boring—and that is a miracle!"

Now the water flowed out and filled the lake. Now it flows as a little stream; now it splashes in the Fountain of the Father's Goodness on Canaan; and in times of drought it irrigates the whole land, so that it is not only a promised land, but also a goodly land, green and blossoming as faith had seen it while it was still a "desert"

Sister Anita

The human intellect constructs; it organizes and yet it always reaches the limit of its capabilities just at the point where man's social life begins. All the development of the human mind, the increase of man's intellectual capacity as far as atomic and space research are concerned has not solved the problems of living with one another. On the contrary, this development has only led to the isolation and loneliness of men, to the deepening of differences, indeed to complete hatred and mutual destruction. The Holy Spirit, on the other hand, according to our experience gives something which is not naturally constructed; He gives us the fellowship of the Spirit which the apostle Paul describes in Philippians 2:1 and 2 Corinthians 13:14, which is followed by "affection and sympathy". Over one hundred of us Sisters of Mary live together in close community life—diverse ages, temperaments and characters, from different backgrounds, from different economical, social and cultural traditions, with varying degrees of education and in various fields. Furthermore, our religious background, our denominational preferences and spiritual maturity before joining the Sisterhood of Mary varied widely. And yet we are placed together, although in the natural course of events we would not have chosen one another as friends. Must not many moments of tension arise? Must not barriers be erected between us? Must not understandable reserve cause us to keep our distance? Won't cliques be formed and antipathies spread? From the very beginning we have experienced all of these things—that is to say, we have experienced traces of them.

If there were no Holy Spirit such a community life would become unbearable. But He is there! And we have experienced something of the miracle of Pentecost among the early Christians: "They devoted themselves to . . . fellowship . . . together" (Acts 2:42,46). What a gift this fellowship in the Spirit is! It is stronger than anything else that can bind us together, whether blood, conviction or common interest.

What welds us together is the grace by which we all live after we have daily received so much forgiveness of sin. To live by forgiveness, to forgive one another and receive forgiveness is the strongest bond of love there is. That creates brotherhood, sisterhood, fellowship. For this reason our meetings for "fellowship in the light"—as we call these family gatherings of the Sisterhood—are the sober basis of our "fellowship in the Spirit"; they are derived from the scripture: "If we walk in the light, as he is in the light, we have fellowship with one another" (1 John 1:7). Sins and errors which concern the whole fellowship are confessed before the fellowship. We ask one another for forgiveness where we have seen our sin. We admonish one another where the individual cannot perceive her own faults or omissions.

When we now look back on twenty years of community life we can do nothing but sing songs of praise. It is incomparably more wonderful today than it was during the revival. These fellowships in light and every inner battle for the unity of the Spirit and of love are rewarded not only in eternity but already here on earth. Despite our weaknesses which continually cause us to fall we nevertheless experience something of the kingdom of heaven in our community life on Canaan. We cannot be away from the fellowship without being homesick; after years abroad or services away from home there is no more joyful moment than that of coming back home to our Mothers and Sisters; and every parting means a painful separation from the spiritual body of the Sisterhood.

Whoever is acquainted with community life, not as an imaginery illusion but as a reality, will understand why we are so astonished and thankful. The daily-experienced miracle can only be due to the working of the Holy Spirit. May He be praised!

Sister Ruth

FOLLOW THIS WAY!

The whole history of our Sisterhood both in its origin and its development over twenty years has wonderfully shown the wise leading of the Holy Spirit.[27] Time and again when we speak of it among the Sisters we can only give thanks and praise Him. There was no beaten track which the Sisterhood of Mary could have travelled safely with the goal in view, but often the path had to be sought in completely unmapped, unexplored country.

Already our previous history gives much evidence of such leading by the Spirit. On the clear direction of the Holy Spirit both of us who were later to become the leaders were in 1935 enabled to brace the step of giving up our professions, leaving Hamburg without means of support and in

110

Darmstadt plunging into a life completely devoid of security or meaning! Nobody could have guessed that in 1936 a small girls' Bible study would gather under our leadership or that this class would later have any importance or that the Sisterhood of Mary would grow out of it.

Through a similar leading Mother Martyria was directed in March, 1945 to travel with fifteen girls of our Bible class to a retreat—in spite of low-level bombing and continuous air-raid warnings and the imminent, hourly-expected entry of American troops into Darmstadt and in spite of her own most severe temptations. Something decisive for our whole future work was to be laid down and effected in those days of inner preparation. The spiritual basis for priestly living in love towards Jesus was revealed.

By the direction of the Holy Spirit it was clear to us that from the beginning we were to go the way of faith for our whole work. So we were never to look to men for the great sums necessary for our mission, not even by way of payment for services rendered, but only to God alone. This method was quite contrary to our dispositions, contrary to reason and also to the opinions of close friends. Still we were to follow this road of faith though it be bitterly hard. The extent of such dependence and uncertainty resulting from it must bring suffering. To the extent that this way makes us small, God is glorified. Today it is in this road of faith that the great answer to the "God is dead" theology is to be found. We were continually dependent upon the leading of the Spirit, for our path was surrounded by pitfalls and could branch out in many different directions. From all sides we heard,

111

"here's the right way for you", "—join us!", "—dedicate yourselves to this or that work! That is God's will for you Sisters." How easy it is to be led astray by the very reasonableness of these well-meaning voices! If we had simply looked after the sick, then all at once we would have made many friends. Had we consistently ordered our financial affairs in the usual way, we would no longer have needed to take this obscure walk of faith on the brink of a precipice. Had we done social work, there would have been fewer opponents. We would have been generally recognised and even supported from official sources . . . It was only the Holy Spirit who steered us past these rocks, who made us cling to the God-given way with our distinctive commission and gave us clear insight at every cross-road.

Through the Holy Spirit's guidance we were also clearly shown our task of proclaiming the call of Jesus, "Repent, for the kingdom of God is at hand", not only by work but by life, the life of our fellowship. We were to try to live together the Sermon on the Mount and to bring Jesus' preaching of the kingdom of God on earth into the fullest possible corporeal reality. We were to walk together in the light and be a Sisterhood of repentance so that once more men may see that where repentance is, life and happiness reign. And in the most materialistic age of history we were to live in personal poverty without salary or possessions as a sign of discipleship and of confidence in the Father.

We were shown in 1955 that God was going to give us a twenty-two acre stretch of land, "Canaan", with buildings for these tasks of ours. Canaan was to be a living expression of the kingdom of God. This land adjoining our Mother House was not available to us at that time. Yet God gave us a clear vision of the future tasks of "Canaan" which has today been fulfilled in every detail. Through this vision He enabled us to take each decisive step.

Indeed, from the beginning our commission was to serve God in prayer and worship and through a ministry of proclamation. So we were led not only to build the Chapel of the Mother House, but also the Herald Chapel and later our Chapels of Praise in Switzerland. Among the countless people out of touch with God were many whom we were to call home through the Herald Plays, through the printed word distributed and broadcast, and in book and pamphlet, through boxes of leaflets and plaques of praise placed at scenic spots, through ministry among holiday-makers at the Chapels of Praise and through the ministry at the Holy Places in the midst of present-day tourism. We were to undertake a service of expiation towards Israel. And Canaan was to be the center for all this, a place of spiritual renewal with houses for quiet, for equipment for everyday life and for caring for the souls of those who are troubled and sick at heart. So the Holy Spirit not only showed us our own commission but demonstrated its reality through the goodness and omnipotence of God.

Looking back we can only thank God in amazement that for more than twenty years we have been led in the right paths and God has shown us, "This is My path". Many at home and abroad have testified that through this way they came into a deeper love for the Lord and into true Christian discipleship. Of all the miracles so far experienced, this has been for us the greatest, the miracle of the leading and guiding of the Holy Spirit.

Mother Basilea and Mother Martyria

MY HELPER AND ADVISER

I hardly know how to begin to praise the Holy Spirit, when I think of the constant arranging He must do to prepare the mosaic patterns of my daily life. I need Him to a special degree for, as a leader, I am completely dependent upon Him. And when there is a wealth of work, and when the heavy pressures of responsibility add their burden, the Holy Spirit alone sees me through. I continually experience His help as the "paraclete", the "One called to stand alongside".

Every morning I ask Him earnestly for His leading and guidance. Then it is as if there were someone standing beside me and speaking to me, and yet I hear no voice: Now do this!—Stop doing that now!—Tackle this work later!—Now go there!—In the evening the task which seemed almost insurmountable in the morning has been carried through with ease, and my heart is once more full of thanks to the Holy Spirit, for how would the days pass without Him? Burdened with cares, following false trails, I would do what was not according to God's will and would not do what God finds necessary and urgent. It would all be confusion and waste, rush and futility. The result would be irritation, and there would be no blessing on the work. What a gift! We can trust in the Holy Spirit and leave the guidance to Him.

Mother Basilea

How the Holy Spirit penetrates the "world" in a practical manner may be illustrated by the so-called "ministry of praise". Since a few years ago hundreds of places of proclamation and praise have come into being—here in Germany, in other European countries, in .the United States, in the Near East—in the holy places even as far as Sinai. Mountain pastures, the highest summits of the Swiss Alps and Scandinavian fjords now have so-called Places of Praise. They consist of at least a plaque bearing a text but are only complete when they are accompanied by a box of literature—and above all, someone who faithfully prays for and looks after the place.

A Canaan Friend who cares for such a place in the Palatinate uses up to ten thousand tracts a month in his box during the summer months, and at the most he finds 0.02% thrown away. Imagine the volume of God's seed-corn which is broadcast through three hundred existing boxes with many more continually coming into existence! Must not our hearts be full of praise and thanks to the Holy Spirit, who commissioned us and showed us the way?

"Whose idea was it?" we are often asked. It was revealed through the Holy Spirit, who made us painfully aware that God the Father receives so little praise in His creation. For two years Mother Basilea kept asking us whether we had finally come up with any ideas which could be put into practice. But precisely because we Sisters of Mary proved to be so helpless in this matter and had not found any ways, we can only praise His achievement.

It was He, the Spirit of God, who instructed us that this was a divine commission. When we made what seemed like senseless experiments at first, fresh guidance from the Spirit always came and He showed us at every stage what needed to be done next in order to draw people's attention to the Creator in the midst of the creation through visible signs, that is to say through these plaques of praise. So it was the Spirit of faith who overcame the hindrances and prepared many secular authorities and officials to allow God's proclamation on these plaques to be mounted in their territories.

Sister Cornelia

WHAT NOBODY COULD HAVE GUESSED

Those whose work lies in the realm of spiritual counselling will not be spared difficult problems. For years I have been serving on the housing projects in our evangelistic work. A heavily burdened girl who from childhood had lived a very sinful life had brought me to the limits of my ability to help. When she spoke, she told me completely false fantasies—when it came to admission of guilt, she was silent and spoke not a word for ten or twenty minutes.

Was it that she couldn't, or wouldn't? I sat there helpless. But then I prayed and listened inwardly to see if the Holy Spirit could help me further. And He did. He gave me the questions which required only 'yes' or 'no' from the girl, and through this came the beginning of redemption for her. I shall never forget how once I could think of nothing more to ask and yet felt that a heavy sense

116

of guilt was burdening the girl. Then like lightning the Holy Spirit caused me to remember a confession that I had heard many years before from another person—and I suggested this same thing to the girl to her face with a sureness of aim that did not come from me. It hit the mark. This was exactly what had been burdening her. She found release when she was able to admit 'Yes!' She went away freed after prayer and forgiveness and with a new faith and power to fight against sin.

Sister Jochebed

THE DICTIONARY AND SINGLE-HEARTED LOVE FOR CHRIST

If you become a Sister of Mary when you are no longer very young, after having done church work for many years, actively taking part in all of the events of the church—both inwardly and outwardly—you bring a well-rounded knowledge of the Bible. At least you think you do. But probably you have not noticed how much you can miss in reading and hearing the Word of God for years. It is possible that you have basically understood very little about the call and demands of Jesus. In any case, I was firmly convinced that I had a wide general understanding of spiritual knowledge and doctrine when I entered the Sisterhood of Mary.

Very soon, however, I seemed to be treading new ground. One of the first words which had hitherto been unknown in my outward as well as my inward vocabulary and which I now met was "bridal love", that single-hearted love for Jesus like that of a bride. I had in fact come across it previously on one occasion when I was studying church history, and had looked it up in a theological dictionary. There "bridal love" was explained as a medieval phenomenon, belonging to the past and having no present significance for myself or the church.

What I now saw, heard and experienced was a warm, fresh, bubbling spring, full of joy and life, for "to love Jesus is to call the fairest treasure of heaven and earth one's one", and one can have this treasure now, today, present and alive. The Holy Spirit brought God's Word to life for me. Verses like "you shall love the Lord your God with all your heart, and with all your soul, and with all your mind" (Matt. 22:37), Jesus' parables of the treasure hidden in the field and the pearl of great price took on new meaning for me, a radiance they had never before had. All Jesus' teaching about renunciation, sacrifice and leaving all to follow Him, presupposes one thing, that my whole love belongs to Him for whose sake I count all else as loss.

It took some time to grasp all this. Scales did not suddenly fall from my eyes, but more and more I recognised that "the faithful shall live with Him in love". This teaching of the Holy Spirit was so strong and His lessons so convincing and authoritative that my heart was gripped more and more by this single-hearted love for Jesus, and I came to experience the truth of Mother Basilea's words from her little booklet "the Grace of Love", "to love Jesus means to bear His Name in our hearts as the joyful secret of a bride."

Sister Fidelis

Isn't it necessary to have read or at least to have handled every important new publication? Oughtn't we as far as possible to see for ourselves what is under discussion in contemporary art, theatre and film? Ought we not to become involved deeply in the prevailing manner of life in order to share the experience of contemporary man and be able to communicate with him? Surely yes! And once I would readily have answered 'yes'.

But meanwhile I have had a new insight. The Holy Spirit at any rate often works in a different, and entirely opposite way. It is good that He does so! Otherwise we would be positively enslaved by the tremendous volume of the often negative cultural output of our day. Yet there is a certain value in the acquisition of information which is not to be disparaged. It should only be said tht nobody need fear that he will lose touch with present-day trends if he lives a life which concentrates entirely on the Gospel. Nobody who gives prayer the first priority will lose touch with the problems of his day, for he will receive practical guidance from another source. Indeed, the Holy Spirit will, with reference to a slender measure of information, give a knowledge, a breadth of view and foresight such as no human source of information could bring about. For the Holy Spirit is in touch with contemporary events.

Here are a few examples:

When in 1962 the Cuban crisis struck the world and drove the Christian church afresh into prayer, we had just in the preceeding months, under a strong inward compulsion, produced a litany for times of special need, a prayer for gracious protection from the dangers of nuclear war "Let not the sword of judgment fall, in Thy mercy give Thy people further years of grace." In October the text was ready and in the press. So this prayer was ready to use just when the Cuban crisis had given many in the church a fresh jolt, shaking them up to their responsibility for effective prayer in times of special world need. The Holy Spirit is in touch with contemporary events.

Another example of the Holy Spirit's working was the Herald-Play "The Time is Near". As a gift of the Holy Spirit the text was written within the span of a few short hours. We felt constrained to alter the advertised schedule for the year 1961 and to include this play. It then became the main play for 1962. In the summer months of these two years thousands heard the choirs singing "The hour of His wrath has come to destroy those who have destroyed the earth . . . Sons of men wake up! . . ." and had heard the dialogues which brought the Word of God into relationship with the nuclear age. They had thus been called upon not to miss the voice of God in historic events—as it was so seriously expressed through the Cuban crisis. The Holy Spirit is in touch with contemporary events.

When the lawlessness began to erupt in our nation, it was my task to read various daily papers and to pass on the news to the rest of the Sisterhood. Mother Basilea told me that she felt that I was missing the significant news. I did not understand this at the time and thought that I was being very careful and that a bank-robbery or murder was scarcely worth mentioning—for had these not taken place all the time?

I did not understand the situation until later when it had already hit the headlines in the newspapers and magazines. But even before that time Mother Basilea could not dispel her inner disquiet. In the Spirit she felt the inroads of the powers of darkness, which later the statistics so clearly confirmed. Out of this unrest which she received from the Spirit, the book "And None Would Believe It" was written and immediately translated into six European languages because it was so up-to-date. The Holy Spirit is in touch with contemporary events.

When the pamphlets in the series, "A Word for Our Time", came out with their quite specific challenge for each year's particular situation, many of our guests said, or readers wrote to us, "How is it possible for you to grasp that so clearly. I am out in the world and yet my eyes were first opened through these writings!" Since then, I have seen what it all depends on, that only he who spends much time in prayer can react quickly and live and act in touch with the present time, for God's Spirit speaks to him in the silence, and shows him what needs to be said at the time. The Holy Spirit is always in touch with contemporary life.

Sister Rebekka

CUE FOR THE 'REVOLVING STAGE'

Some time ago Mother Martyria passed on to us a tested and original remedy against every kind of bitterness and enmity and judgment of others.

"When somebody has hurt me or done me an injustice so that the memory of it keeps rising up in me, I instantly ask the Holy Spirit to turn my revolving stage round again and He does so every time. Then the actor who has held the stage hitherto, my guilty, misbehaving neighbour, fades suddenly into the background, and I with my guilt and wrong attitude come into the foreground. With this change of scene produced by the Holy Spirit, there also comes about a reversal of the question of guilt, for I am suddenly the principal sinner and the other who disappeared from the stage is no longer so important. It is no longer difficult to forgive him because so much must now be forgiven me "

For me this was just the right advice, for I had often been unable to see any way out when I could not detect the 'beam' in my own eye. Meanwhile, I have tried out this advice and can testify that the Spirit of truth does just this for us when we ask Him and persevere until it comes to pass, even though it may cost hours of prayer.

Sister Laurentia

THOU DOST LIGHT MY LAMP

I had only been in the Sisterhood of Mary for a year and had many inward battles to fight. While I was in my former profession I had been considered clever. But now I had come into a new class in God's school, which is described by Kierkegaard's statement: "Whatever God wishes to use He first reduces to nothing." Many know these dark hours. I felt uncertain in many ways and was disheartened.

One Sunday we young Sisters had quiet meditation. But I did not know how I should pray. Everything was so dark. The only thing that was clear to me was that my needs could only be solved by prayer. So I went once more into the "Herald Chapel" where many visitors had sat that afternoon at a Passion Play. I sat down, depressed, in the choir loft where once I had loved to pray, and looked up at the crucifix just barely visible in the twilight. I only longed to be rid of this inner paralysis. Then the words from the Bible that I had read in my morning devotion were fulfilled, "Thou dost light my lamp; the Lord my God lightens my darkness" (Psa.18:28). Without any act of will I began to sing in a language and melody which I myself did not know—there was no effort involved—it was as if I were only listening. I went on for perhaps an hour and felt everything that was included in this prayer: worship, thanksgiving, petition and intercession which burst the bonds of my own heart and reached even further than the aim of my heart, which up until then had been so sad.

What a blessing this gift of singing and praying in other tongues was for me just at the time when I could no longer pray in my own strength!

A Sister of Mary

CHARISMA—A GIFT!

A Jewish friend had received as a small present when he stayed with us a photograph of the bas-relief of the offering of Isaac which a few years earlier I had made for the Moriah memorial in

Wustenrot. He was himself an artist and took the picture to his friends in the Artists' Guild in Israel, asking them to guess who had done it. They guessed this and that, were full of admiration and unaminous in thinking that in any case it must have been the work of a great master. When his letter was read aloud at table, I had to smile—I did not yet know that great masters and poor-but-gifted sinners could be alike in their work.

I had in fact begun with great zeal as an art student and intended to go all out to become a professional artist. Instead of this, however, I was gripped by Jesus, placed by Him in the Sisterhood of Mary and put into the school of the Holy Spirit. Thereupon my career ran rapidly down hill. For years I did not do any artistic work. When I was asked to take it up again, nothing went right for me. Even the most sympathetic of people could not praise my work! I no longer had the courage to attempt new tasks. When Mother Martyria walked with me across Canaan—at that time it was still a chaos of untidy sandhills—she described to me how she imagined the layout of our "Garden of Jesus' Sufferings", which was planned as a prayer garden. In this corner there was to be a relief, and over there a sculpture, and there an Easter mosaic. But in me there was nothing but despair. So much of what I had created had obviously not been of the Holy Spirit.

Then came the moment when I had to begin the shaping of the "Garden of Jesus' Sufferings" and something remarkable happened. Instead of my 'I cannot', the pictures of the individual places of His suffering stood before me—I fashioned them while God's Spirit helped me to find the form and shape.

124

I discovered what a "gift" is—what it means to receive something which is literally given! Perhaps this is why the sculptures in this garden, although in no way meeting the requirements of modern man, nevertheless move so many.

Thanks be to the Lord, the Holy Spirit, who destroys the natural before He bestows His gifts!

Sister Myrrhia

I AM NOT AN EYE!

In our nursery hung a childrens' calendar from "Bethel" and while my hair was being plaited I always read the tear-off for the day. On these there was often something about the feeble-minded children and adults at "Bethel", about cripples, about the underprivileged. The Holy Spirit used these stories to awaken in me a great love for such people—to sow the seed of the charisma of service in my heart.

Later I belonged to a youth-group. In it were some very intelligent girls who could sing in parts and even sight-read. They also already had the gift of leading Bible studies and giving testimonies, and I felt myself quite outdone by them. I was not musical; I was quiet and not so good at speaking; and so I began to suffer from feelings of inferiority. One day when I was struggling with this problem, the leader of the group took me on one side and told me what pride and ingratitude this was, and that I must repent of it. She asked me if I knew the text, "as each has received a gift, employ it for one another", I had not yet noticed that I had been given a quite different gift by the Holy

Spirit. I could always make immediate contact with the less bright girls in the group. Because of certain differences of talent and education, there was a gap between them and the secondary school girls which I was able to bridge, because the Holy Spirit had given me a love precisely for those who belong more to the "poor" of the world, whose confidence I always gained.

Later, when I was at work, a colleague once said to me "I'm going to have a notice posted on your door saying, 'rubbish dump' ", because those of my fellow workers who were refugees or otherwise in need always tried to unburden their hearts there.

In the Sisterhood of Mary I was given the pastoral care of the women in prison and also of the aged and sick in a home. In this I was always conscious that this was a gift of the Holy Spirit to be daily renewed so that I could simply use it in His service and He could work through it. Since then I no longer envy anybody 'above' me, for "if the ear should say, because I am not an eye, I do not belong to the body, that would not make it any less a part of the body" (1 Cor.12:16).

Sister Stephana

THE GIFT OF INTERPRETATION

Just at a time when we Sisters of Mary were reaching out full of longing towards the Holy Spirit and the renewal of His gifts among us, I felt my "stony heart" more than ever. I felt no breath of new spiritual life in me. Everything was flat. At the same time, however, I did not know what the cause of this condition might be. So I simply held out and asked the Lord not to let me be a drag on the fellowship or on our commission. In the midst of this time of inner poverty and dryness, I received one day the gift of interpretation. When in times of prayer together some Sisters spoke or sang in tongues, I understood the meaning and obediently undertook to convey what I understood. It encouraged me that this agreed with another Sister's interpretation. For me it was a miracle that I too should be taken up into worship and adoration. It was as if iron fetters were removed from my heart—and when sometimes I went into such an evening worship in a depressed state it happened that the prayers which I heard and interpreted brought new joy and stimulation to me too. In the quiet time afterwards I could meditate on these things even further and could really pray.

Here also I recognised that God's heart always has loving thoughts. He bestows the gifts expressly for service only—but when we serve Him with them, He strengthens and refreshes His children at the same time.

A Sister of Mary

JOYFUL SINGING AND LAMENTING

Singing in the Spirit can sometimes be a "lament", when the suffering of God moves our hearts. But when it is a matter of joy in God, thanksgiving, praise and adoration, it is a joyful, blessed glorification of the Lord. A priest in Jerusalem once said "It sounds like the piping of the shepherds on our fields at Bethlehem."

This charisma was given to us Sisters of Mary in

a particularly difficult year in which we had experienced something of the wrath of God. At that time the Lord had to correct us on many points, and thus we learned to lament over our sins as was once said by the prophets, "teach to your daughters a lament, and each to her neighbour a dirge" (Jer. 9:20). And we learned to lament over God's suffering because of us. But when this time of God's special correction and chastisement slowly came to an end, an inexpressible joy broke out among us—without noise, a silent, deeply-felt joy at the grace and mercy of God. With this joy, the Spirit of God awakened in us this singing adoration which we, like the priest on the shepherds' field, call joyful singing. We can often spend much time together—whether all of us are there or just a few. Everyone joins softly in the common worship. Each one sings in her own language and melody, yet it is a great single harmony. For us it is a foretaste of heaven.

Often it is children who are most sensitive to what comes from God. We shall never forget the time we performed a Herald Play at a Gospel tent mission in Cologne. Above the crowd of several hundred people a child in his mother's arms began to shout with joy, when we began to worship by singing in the Spirit.

Sister Martina

HEALED!

When I was about three years old, I became very ill with a high temperature and had to be taken to

128

the hospital. When the doctors had finally found the cause and called in a specialist, it was too late. He diagnosed kidney trouble and gave me up as a hopeless case, because I was too small and weak for an operation. My parents took me home with them, the mark of death already upon me. Just at that moment the local vicar came to visit us and told us he was holding a mission in his church and that the missioner had the gift of healing through the laying on of hands. Through his prayer of faith many had already been healed. Immediately my parents put me back into the car and drove me to this man. From the very moment of his laying on of hands, I began to recover. The fever left me. I once more wanted to eat and after a few days I had fully recovered. My parents took me back to the specialist who had given me up for dead. He could not believe his eyes, nor grasp what had happened, but all tests and X-rays were negative. He could only conclude that this was an inexplicable temporary remission and maintained that I would always be liable to kidney trouble recurring through the years. But since then over thirty years have passed and I have never had any kidney trouble.

At that time my parents promised that, in the event of my recovery, I would be wholly dedicated to the Lord. Perhaps this is why He did not let me go, but later called me quite personally into His keeping, into the Sisterhood of Mary. For this I am deeply grateful.

Sister Caecilie

FOOTNOTES

[1] Missionary Detmar Scheunemann, Institute Indjil Indonesia, Batu (Malang), Indonesia, personal conversation.

[2] Friedrich Zuendel, *Joh. Christoph Blumhardt*, Brunnen-Verlag, Giessen, 1962, p. 143

[3] Ralf Luther, *Neutestamentliches Woerterbuch*, Furche-Verlag, Hamburg, 1951, p. 49. (*New Testament Dictionary*)

[4] *ibid.*, p. 50, 210.

[5] Werner Meyer, "Der erste Brief an die Korinther", 2. Teil, *Schweizerisches Bibelwerk fuer die Gemeinde*, Zwingli-Verlag, Zurich, p. 117. ("The First Letter to the Corinthians", Part Two, *Swiss Bible Reference Book for Church Use*)

[6] Ludwig Albrecht, Uebersetzung des Neuen Testaments mit Erlaeuterungen, Commentary for I Corinthians 12:10. (Translation of the New Testament with Notes)

[7] *op. cit.*, Luther, p. 211.

[8] *ibid.*, p. 50.

[9] Joseph Brosch, *Charismen und Aemter in der Urkirche*, Bonn, p. 50. (*The Charismata and Administrations in the Early Church*)

[10] *op. cit.*, Meyer, p. 194f.

[11] *ibid.*, p. 195ff., 122.

[12] *ibid.*, p. 198.

[13] *ibid.*, p. 104.

[14] *ibid.*, p. 124, 120, 125.

[15] G. v. Bodelschwingh, *F. v. Bodelschwingh—ein Lebensbild*, Bethel bei Bielefeld, 1922, p. 278, 311. (*F. v. Bodelschwingh—a Life Sketch*)

[16] Dr. H. and G. Taylor, *Hudson Taylor—ein Lebensbild*, II. Band, China-Inland-Mission, Merlingen, 1948, p. 317f. (*Hudson Taylor —a Life Sketch*, Vol. II.)

[17] Joh. Warneck, *D. Nommensen—ein Lebensbild*, Verlag des Missionshauses, Wuppertal-Barmen, 1943, p. 38. (D' Nommensen—a Life Sketch)

[18] *op. cit.*, Zuendel, p. 162.

[19] *op. cit.*, Luther, p. 211.

[20] Michael Harper, *As at the Beginning*, Hodder & Stoughton, London, 1965, p. 71.

[21] Sadhu Sundar Singh, *Gesammelte Schriften*, Evang. Missionsverlag, Stuttgart, 1951, p. 15, 205. (*Collected works*)

[22] David Wilkerson, *The Cross and the Switchblade*, Lakeland, London, 1964, p. 164ff.

[23] Missionary Detmar Scheunemann, Institute Indjil Indonesia, Batu (Malang), Indonesia, personal conversation.

[24] Karl Heim, *Gemeinde des Auferstandenen*, Munich, 1949, p. 207f. (*Church of the Risen Lord*)

[25] O.S. v. Bibra, *Der Name Jesus*, Brockhaus-Verlag, Wuppertal, 1961, p. 49. (*The Name Jesus*)

[26] See further details in *Realities: The Miracles of God Experienced Today*, Basilea Schlink, Lakeland, London, 1967.

[27] Further details in *God is Always Greater* by Basilea Schlink, (Faith Press, London) and in *Realities* (Lakeland, London).